Conscious Breathing

BY GAY HENDRICKS

The Centering Book (with Russel Wills)

Learning to Love Yourself

The Learning to Love Yourself Workbook

BY GAY HENDRICKS AND KATHLYN HENDRICKS

At the Speed of Life

Centering and the Art of Intimacy

Conscious Loving

Radiance! Breathwork, Movement and Body-Centered Psychotherapy

Conscious Breathing

BREATHWORK for HEALTH, STRESS RELEASE, and PERSONAL MASTERY

Gay Hendricks, Ph.D.

BANTAM BOOKS

New York   Toronto   London   Sydney   Auckland

Conscious Breathing
A Bantam Book/April 1995
All rights reserved.
Copyright © 1995 by Gay Hendricks, Ph.D.

BOOK DESIGN BY GLEN M. EDELSTEIN
INTERIOR ILLUSTRATIONS BY WENDY WRAY

Hendricks, Gay.
Conscious breathing / Gay Hendricks.
p.   cm.
Includes bibliographical references.
ISBN 0-553-37443-5
I. Breathing exercises. I. Title.
RA782.H46   1995
613'.192—dc20   94-30387
CIP

Published simultaneously in the United States and Canada

Bantam Books are published by Bantam Books, a division of Bantam Doubleday Dell Publishing
Group, Inc. Its trademark, consisting of the words "Bantam Books" and the portrayal of a rooster,
is Registered in U.S. Patent and Trademark Office and in other countries. Marca Registrada.
Bantam Books, 1540 Broadway, New York, New York 10036.

Printed in the United States of America

FFG   0 9 8 7 6 5 4 3 2 1

To
WILHELM REICH
and
MOSHE FELDENKRAIS,
two pioneers of twentieth-century body-centered transformation

CONTENTS

THREE: CONSCIOUS BREATHING FOR SPECIAL CONCERNS

The Breath Test

Find Out in a Minute
If You Need Conscious Breathing

Take a moment to answer these twelve questions:

- When you take a deep breath, do you inflate your chest?
- Do you tire easily or wake up tired?
- Do you experience racy or mildly queasy sensations in your chest or stomach?
- Do you often feel that you are not getting a full breath?
- Do you get mild or more severe headaches, often in the afternoon?
- Is your breathing shallow?
- Is your breath mostly up in your chest?
- Are your muscles often tense or sore to the touch?
- Do you sigh often?
- Do you sometimes have painful sensations in your rib cage or shooting pains that make you want to hold your breath?
- Do you feel breathless fairly often?
- In repose, do you breathe more than fifteen times a minute?

All of these symptoms can be caused by ineffective breathing. All of them can disappear as you learn to breathe more effectively. If you answered yes to any of these questions, you can benefit from the practices in this book. If you answered yes to three or more, you will find the activities extremely useful, perhaps even life-changing.

Beginning a Breath-Taking Journey to Wholeness

I FEEL DEEPLY PRIVILEGED TO BE WRITING THIS BOOK. For about half my life now I have been directly engaged in helping people learn to feel better through conscious breathing. Throughout this time I have been my own best customer. I have benefited in every imaginable way from the ideas and processes I will share with you in this book. To bring what I know about breathing to you is the culmination of a life dream.

When I began my career, there was little information on breathwork. In fact, I think I may have coined the term. I began using it in the early seventies to denote the conscious use of breathing as a tool for healing, stress reduction, and personal development. In breathwork, the practitioner uses awareness of breathing and a variety of specific techniques to accomplish the same aims for which verbal therapists and conventional healers use talk and medicine. It is my conviction that breathwork will play an

He lives most life whoever breathes most air.
—ELIZABETH BARRETT BROWNING

Breathing, you invisible poem!
World-space constantly in pure
interchange with our own being. Counterpoise,
wherein I rhythmically happen.
—RAINER MARIA RILKE

enormous role in both medicine and psychotherapy in the twenty-first century. Nowadays I tend to use the phrase *conscious breathing* as a substitute for *breathwork*. The reason is that I have grown to feel uncomfortable with the "work"part of breathwork. Breathwork is really breath*play* in its finest form, not work at all. In this book I will use the terms *breathwork* and *conscious breathing* interchangeably.

The use of breathing as a transformative tool has a long and rich tradition. References to it in the spiritual traditions go back several thousand years. In modern times we have rediscovered its power, putting it to work to enhance well-being in a variety of areas. What you have in your hands is the distillation of my experience in finding out what works and refining it. I make no claim to having invented anything at all about breathing. Furthermore, I would regard as arrogant anyone who made such a claim. Conscious breathing is everyone's birthright, and my contribution is to refine the essence of breathing practices into a practical program that anyone can use every day.

You do not have to adopt any esoteric belief system to benefit from this program. I have met many people who rejected breathing practices because they came laden with excess philosophical baggage and cultish claptrap. This program requires no changes in belief, diet, or lifestyle. To paraphrase a popular sneaker advertisement, you just have to do it. You may become a true believer, as I have, in the power of these practices, but it will be a belief founded entirely on your own experience.

Twenty years ago, when I first began to study breathing and use it in therapy, my skeptical colleagues would sometimes snicker at my enthusiasm. "You've got to try these techniques,"I would urge. "They are going to revolutionize the field."I must admit that I was obnoxious in my zeal when I first discovered the power of breathwork. Like many new converts, I was on fire with my new understanding, and I wanted the rest of the world to catch fire, too. Even though I have tempered some of my early evangelical zeal, I actually feel more enthusiastic now than I did when I began in the early seventies. But today it is definitely getting harder to find skeptics. Now, after several hundred studies of the effectiveness of breathwork in treating a host of psychological and medical ills, the scientific community has verified what the community of therapists has discovered: Breathwork works.

BREATHWORK IS MOVING TOWARD THE MAINSTREAM

During the past fifteen years out on the lecture circuit I have often crossed paths with Andrew Weil, M.D. Our meetings usually consist of a five-minute chat in the hall at a conference where we are both speaking. Andy is one of the most broadly educated people I have ever met, and one of the most open-minded. His Harvard Medical School education gave him a rigorous immersion in the Western medical model, but he did not stop there. He has studied herbs, psychoactive plants, acupuncture, osteopathy, and a dozen other healing arts. He is interested in discovering what works, not in protecting his belief system. When I see him, the first thing I usually ask him is, "What are you most interested in these days?" It was with enormous satisfaction not long ago that I heard him say that one of his current hot interests was in the therapeutic use of breathing! His interest is mirrored by many other people on the leading edge of the healing community. It was his opinion, as it is mine, that breathwork is heading toward a secure place in the mainstream of healing and personal growth.

    Many people now are seeking organic ways to heal themselves and feel good. Prescription drugs, necessary though they may be in many

Our breathing is the fragile vessel that carries us from birth to death.
—DR. FREDERICK LEBOYER

The Latin word for breath is *spiritus*. Allow your breath to flow through you as a sense of spirit flows through your body.
—JERRY BRAZA, PH.D.

circumstances, are powerful also in their side effects. Recreational drugs are losing favor among the thoughtful because the feelings of well-being they may produce come at a cost, sometimes fatal. Even if there were no costly side effects, the health-conscious person would eventually want to find a permanent, beneficial aid to health and consciousness. Breathwork is the ideal alternative. It is free and completely within our conscious control. For these reasons, and because of its power, breathwork deserves to become a major healing art. There are those of us, still few but growing in number, who believe that breathwork will ultimately rise in popularity to become the predominant healing technology of our time.

A COMPREHENSIVE HEALING TOOL

I am deeply grateful to the power of conscious breathing for what it has brought to me personally and to the thousands of clients with whom I have used it. I use it every day in my own quest for health, and I use it in every session with psychotherapy clients. About a hundred days a year I also teach it to audiences of professionals who want to put it to work in their practices. I have taught it in Europe, Asia, and North America. Whether I am in Prague or Kalamazoo, I find that breathwork bridges cultural barriers more effectively than anything else I have seen.

There is a Hawaiian word—*ohana*—that in its contemporary usage means "family." Its older meaning encompassed a wider community, literally "people who breathe together." When the missionaries came to the islands, the natives called them *haoles*, which translates, unflatteringly, as "people without breath."

In the wake of the recent dissolution of the Soviet bloc, I have received letters from people in the Czech Republic, Bulgaria, and Russia who want to learn about breathwork. As one person in Croatia put it in a deeply moving letter, "Finally after forty years of restriction, we can breathe freely. Now we want to learn how to breathe effectively."

If this is your desire, I congratulate you for it. It is a profoundly interesting and healthful path. Welcome to our large and growing *ohana*.

> I add my breath to your breath
> That our days may be long on the Earth
> That the days of our people may be long
> That we may be one person . . .
>
> ANCIENT KERES SONG,
> TRANSLATED BY PAULA GUNN ALLEN

PART I

The Breath of Life

CHAPTER 1

Well-Being of Mind, Body, and Spirit

Eight Reasons to Practice Conscious Breathing

THERE ARE MANY REASONS WHY I PRACTICE CONSCIOUS BREATHING and recommend it to my friends and clients. Some of the reasons are practical, some mystical. Breathing has the power to enhance both the practical present moment and our mystical connection with infinity. It is all there in the breath, free for the asking.

Breath is so vital to life that to go without it for even a very short time is fatal. The average person can go without food for several weeks, without liquid for several days. But oxygen is a different matter entirely. If you close off the oxygen supply to your brain by pressing the pulse points on the sides of your neck, reality as you know it starts to melt down rapidly. I have done this experimentally on several occasions and have been amazed at how quickly my consciousness changes. There are about ten seconds of gathering mistiness, followed very shortly by utter panic. After

To our ordinary consciousness, breathing only serves to maintain our body. But if we go beyond our mind, breathing can open up a completely new foundation for our life.
—ILSA MIDDENDORF

four minutes or so without oxygen, your brain will never work the same again.

Since yesterday at this time you have taken perhaps twenty thousand breaths. In your lifetime you will breathe in and out more than a hundred million times. Given the sheer volume, it is very easy to take breathing for granted, to assign it to the deep background of life. But what if you made a tiny improvement in something you did that many times? If you can learn to breathe even a little bit better, you will notice immediate, profound shifts in your physical, mental, and emotional well-being. If you learn to breathe effectively, you will improve the quality of your entire life.

A BREATH OF FRESH AIR

Follow with me the miraculous journey of a breath of fresh air as it makes its way into your system. Darwin is said to have shuddered when he contemplated the complexity of the eye. No less thrilling are the exquisite and delicately balanced mechanisms of breathing. When I began to understand the miracle that takes place on every breath, I found myself taking even more pleasure in my breathing.

If you are breathing correctly, air begins its life-giving journey by entering your nose. While resting in bed, you inhale about eight quarts of air a minute. Just sitting up doubles your requirement to sixteen quarts a minute. If you go jogging, you will bring in fifty quarts of air a minute. A strong argument can be made for nose-breathing, even in athletic exertion. The air we breathe is only about 20 percent oxygen. There is a tiny amount of carbon dioxide in it, less than one percent, and the rest is nitrogen. But each in-breath also brings with it a swarm of irritants, pollu-

The smoke of my own breath,
echoes, ripples, buzz'd whispers,
love-root, silk-thread,
crotch and vine,
my respiration and inspiration,
the beating of my heart,
the passing of blood and air
through my lungs . . .
—WALT WHITMAN

tants, and dust. The nose has a set of filters designed for clearing the larger particles of dust from the air as it heads toward the lungs. Your mouth is not equipped for filtering air, being mainly a food-hole rather than an air-hole. You can breathe through your mouth, but as any stuffy-nosed cold-sufferer knows, a little bit of it goes a long way. Apparently mouth-breathing was so common a habit in the nineteenth century that an author named George Catlin wrote a best-seller with the blunt title *Shut Your Mouth!* Writing in the florid style of his time, he attributed a wide variety of physical and moral ills to mouth-breathing. Morality aside, the nose is a much better entry point for the breath than its gaping cousin to the south.

As air enters the nose, it first encounters a tiny but important set of filters that we can observe as we look in the mirror and tilt our heads back: nose hairs. These hairs offer the first line of resistance to the pollutants and dust particles that float in on a wave of fresh air. After breezing through this little thicket, the air passes a veritable Venus flytrap, the mucus blanket that lines the septum, which separates the nostrils. This sticky substance is designed to trap more dust but to allow the air to flow past freely.

For every in-breath there is an out-breath, and as these two currents meet in the nose, a fine microclimate is set up. Moisture is deposited by the out-breath on the mucus blanket, only to be picked up by the entering in-breath. The in-rushing currents of air grow warmer and more moist as they travel through the hair and past the mucus wall. In a miracle of heat-efficiency, the air reaches body temperature within a little more than an inch of the outside world, even on a cold day. At the top end of the nostril, the air enters the turbinate, a narrower passage that brings the air toward the trachea. The mucous membranes that we first encountered in the nasal cavity run the length of the trachea all the way down to the bronchi

Suck space, mouth-breather!
—COMIC-BOOK HERO TO ALIEN INVADER,
AS HE THROWS THE ALIEN OUT
OF THE SPACESHIP

Viruses and microbes live best in low oxygen environments. They are anaerobic. That means, raise the oxygen environment around them and they die.
—Edward McCabe

of the lungs. Most of us know the painful sensation of the mucous membranes when they are inflamed, when a cold makes every breath an unpleasant experience. Most of the time, though, this structure is painlessly doing its job, trapping finer particles of dust and giving a home to thousands of tiny hairlike structures called cilia. Like a field of seaweed, these cilia are in constant motion.

And what are they doing, these tiny dancers of the deep? They are engaged in a heroic and thankless task, but one that is absolutely essential for health. They are passing the mucus blanket upward from the lungs, against gravity. Not only is the mucus blanket able to trap particles of dust and debris, but it is also a microbe hunter. It kills unfriendly bugs and drops them overboard toward the stomach, which gives them an acid bath and sends them south. To top it all off, the mucus blanket is richly supplied with white blood cells, providing a long gauntlet of immune-system barriers through which an invading microbe must pass.

The air, growing purer by the inch, sails past these obstructions and into a tough but flexible tube called the trachea. A traveler in a maze of narrowing tunnels, the air then goes into successively smaller passages called the bronchii and the bronchioles, finally reaching home in the tiny sacs of the lung, the alveoli.

The lungs are divided into four lobes, two on each side of the chest, all resting on the diaphragm. So that the lungs may slide around freely in their duties, they are covered by a lining called the pleura, and they are lubricated by a slick substance called surfactant. Down inside the lungs themselves, in the alveoli, a miracle of transformation is taking place. To appreciate the importance of these little sacs, consider the territory they encompass. If you opened them all and spread them out, they would blanket a basketball court. These structures are engaged night and day in a hot and steamy occupation. Here in these tiny carburetors, thousands of gas exchanges are taking place every moment.

Named for grapes because they come in clusters, the alveoli pass oxygen into your blood while the blood passes carbon dioxide back into the alveoli. They are embedded in a network of blood vessels called capillaries. When red blood gets to the alveoli, it releases its carbon dioxide and gathers in fresh oxygen. Oxygenated blood heads toward the heart to be pumped around the body, while the carbon dioxide is given a quick ride out of the body on the out-breath. The oxygen is carried to the cells, which burn it.

After the oxygen has done its vital work and is spent, it finds its way back to the alveoli again. A gust of exhaled air is made of only 14 percent oxygen and 69 percent nitrogen, along with some water vapor and traces of other gases. But the important passenger on this wave of exiting air is carbon dioxide, about 5 percent of the volume. This is the exhaust, the smoggy emission that will quickly poison your system if not completely exhaled.

And here is why conscious breathing can be a lifesaver to some and a benefit to most. Just as a small adjustment in your front wheels can smooth out a rattling journey, a little attention to your breathing goes a long way. If you only practice and master the three foundation lessons from this book you would increase the oxygenation of your body by about 5 percent on each breath. Multiply that times 20,000 a day! A 5 percent increase means that with each twenty breaths you would be getting a bonus lungful of oxygen. By the end of the day, you would have increased the efficiency of your body a thousandfold. No wonder, then, that people who practice the lessons in this book report a large number of benefits.

Perhaps the most frequently reported benefit is that . . .

There are about 75 trillion cells in your body, and they are all breathing—or should be.
—SHELDON SAUL HENDLER, M.D.

CONSCIOUS BREATHING RELEASES STRESS AND TENSION

One of the most important discoveries I have ever made in my own mind and body is how to release tension through healthy breathing. As you will

Just a single thought is capable of changing the breathing pattern.
—ILSE MIDDENDORF

soon see, correct breathing causes tension to melt from your body. It clarifies and focuses your mind at the same time, but its first noticeable effect is likely to be an enhanced feeling of well-being in your body.

Healthy breathing has a direct and immediate effect on stress levels. When at rest, people breathe about 13 times a minute on the average. Men breathe a little more slowly than women, with men's rate being 12 to 14 times a minute compared with 14 to 15 for women. Most of us who work with breathing consider anything above 15 breaths a minute to be a stress signal.

When the human body is under stress, it responds with restricted breathing. The breath becomes shorter, shallower, and more in the chest than in the belly. When the body is relaxed, breathing slows down and drops farther into the belly, becoming deeper and more nurturing. When I explain this to clients, I contrast relaxed breathing with fight-or-flight breathing. Nature has given us two very different breathing patterns, designed for very different situations.

When we perceive a threat, several things happen to our breathing all at once. Our belly muscles tighten, our breath shifts up into the chest, and our breathing speeds up. We are poised to run or fight back. The sympathetic branch of our autonomic nervous system is fired up, dripping adrenaline into our bloodstreams and slowing digestion so that the energy can be diverted to our muscles. When we are no longer perceiving a threat, our breathing shifts from the fight-or-flight pattern to the relaxed pattern. Belly muscles relax, digestion starts again, and the breath drops down into the abdomen. The system goes "off alert," and the parasympathetic branch of the autonomic nervous system begins to take over. All of this can happen in a split second, regardless of whether the threat is a charging rhino or the unexpected midnight creak of a floorboard.

These are automatic responses, wired in by nature over thousands of years of evolution, and they come from deep in the primitive brain. But human beings are endowed with a magnificent cerebral cortex, a structure so complex that it seems magical. The cortex literally surrounds the primitive brain, and it gives us the power to override many of its instructions. We can use the power of our conscious minds to get our breathing to work with us, rather than against us. In other words, human consciousness is powerful enough that we can notice when we are in a stressed breathing pattern and do something about it. We can consciously take deeper, slower breaths, and we can consciously shift our breathing from chest to belly. I have seen this simple but powerful piece of information change many lives.

If you suffer any symptoms of stress in your life, conscious breathing should be a learning priority for you.

Conscious Breathing Builds Energy and Endurance

Modern life makes many demands on us that our forebears did not have to handle. Granted, there were many physical demands and dangers in years gone by, but our modern age has its own special energy drains. It is no surprise that problems like chronic fatigue syndrome are endemic today. One great benefit of conscious breathing is that it has a direct effect on energy level. Put simply, if you breathe effectively you have much more physical energy.

I first spotted this correlation twenty years ago when I was doing a therapy session with a woman in her thirties. She came in for her first session after she had completed her workday. She looked exhausted, and when I said so, she agreed that she was. I asked her to tell me how her day had gone. She told me she had awakened at six that morning to the sound of her baby crying. After nursing the baby, she had fixed breakfast for her

Ninety percent of metabolic oxygen comes from breathing. Ten percent comes from food.
—GABRIEL COUSENS, M.D.

husband and herself, then dashed off to work. (Her husband was not working at the time.) She took the rapid transit to work, put in a full day managing a real estate brokerage, then went back home around four to nurse the baby again. She picked up her car at the shop, bought some groceries, then came by my office for her session.

Now, all that in itself would be enough to make anyone tired, but I noticed something else as she told her story: Her breathing was very shallow, and she actually held her breath when she talked about feeding the baby. I asked her whether there was something upsetting to her about feeding the baby, and she got in touch with feeling conflicted about leaving him every day to go to work. Toward the end of the session I took her through simplified versions of some of the breathing activities you will learn in this book. We rehearsed how she could deepen her breath consciously, particularly at certain times of the day when she felt under the most pressure.

I was gratified to see how she looked when she came in the next week. Even though our session was two hours later in the day than the week before, she looked much peppier. One can never know, of course, whether it was the breathing or the chance to discuss the conflict about her baby that caused the improvement, but the change was clear. She reported a great deal more energy and resilience, which she attributed to remembering to take a few deep breaths throughout the day. Then we turned our attention to a problem as fundamental as her breathing: how to share responsibilities with her husband more equitably.

Many people have reported, and I have also noticed, that conscious breathing produces a steady flow of energy throughout the day. Before I began to practice conscious breathing, my energy was like a roller coaster. When I was high, I felt cheerful and productive, but when I hit a low, I was grouchy, mentally foggy, and physically sluggish. Needless to say, I did not get much productive work done during my down phases. I can date the smoothing out of my roller coaster to the year I began to do two

Breathing is the first place, not the last, one should look when fatigue, disease, or other evidence of disordered energy presents itself.
—SHELDON SAUL HENDLER, M.D.

practices every morning: conscious breathing and meditation. Over the next few years the roller coaster completely disappeared, so that now I cannot even remember what it felt like to have unstable energy.

If fatigue is more than an occasional visitor in your house, I encourage you to make conscious breathing one of your daily priorities.

CONSCIOUS BREATHING CONTRIBUTES TO EMOTIONAL MASTERY

One of the most dramatic applications of conscious breathing is in the emotional realm. I consider the Foundation and Advanced Lessons in this book to be first-line treatments for the two most common emotion-related complaints, anxiety and depression. Although I have tested the lessons with thousands of people with clinical problems (that is, problems serious enough to take to a professional), they work equally well with the milder emotional complaints most of us have from time to time.

The basic emotions that therapists call the Big Three—fear, anger, and sadness—can cause a great deal of trouble for us if we do not know how to deal with them effectively. Here, conscious breathing can be a life-changer. The major problems with feelings is that we tend to ignore them, hide them, or let them linger longer than they need to. Conscious breathing can become a most useful ally in learning to handle emotions.

There is much to learn in the curriculum of emotion. Our traditional education gives us very little help in this area. After all, compared to math, science, and diagramming sentences, how much time did you spend in school learning how to deal with your feelings? For most of us, the answer is zero. Also, for many of us, our families are training grounds for how *not* to handle our emotions.

As one client reports, "I grew up with two alcoholic parents, and my

Fear is excitement without the breath.
—FRITZ PERLS, M.D.

father also sexually molested me. I just thought that was the way it was, and it wasn't until I was in my thirties that I started getting in touch with all the anger and hatred I had felt toward my parents as a child. My therapist kept urging me to feel my anger and learn to express it effectively, but I had absolutely no idea how to do that. My pictures of anger all had to do with my parents exploding and beating me or getting into a screaming match with each other. The rest of the time it was sullen silence. I remember what a tremendous breakthrough it was when I actually let myself feel anger in my body. Then, when I learned to express it, I felt something inside me let go that had been held like a clenched fist for years. The breathing really helped me learn to feel again. I also started noticing that I held my breath instead of saying how I felt to people. This tiny cue helped me learn to notice when I was holding back."

If you observe carefully, you will feel your breathing shift when an emotion is present in your body. A first step to mastery of feelings is simply to notice when you are having one. After working with your breathing for a while, you will likely become more sensitive to shifts in your breathing, so that you will know when an emotion is present. This skill will give you an access to your feelings that can be very helpful in communicating with others.

Breathing also plays a significant role in helping us clear feelings out of our bodies. Once you get the message from a feeling (say, "I'm scared"), you may want to make it disappear. Breathing is the fastest and most effective way to do this. Take a few big breaths into the physical sensations of any emotion, and watch what happens. Many times, that's all it takes to move it out of your body. I have witnessed this done a thousand times now, but it still moves me to see the look on people's faces when they learn that they are the master of their feelings.

Breathing can play a major role in the alleviation of depression. Let me

Emotional and physical states can be altered by changing the breathing pattern.
— WILHELM REICH

give a typical example. A middle-aged woman came for therapy in a state of depression that had been bothering her for several months. She worked for a thoughtful medical doctor who wanted her to explore the problem with a therapist before he put her on an antidepressant. We talked over various issues in the first session, during which I noticed that her breathing was almost completely immobilized. Her abdomen and her chest barely moved when she breathed. She looked as if she were encased in a tight girdle. When I pointed this pattern out to her, she told me she felt that she had not taken a full breath in months. In fact, she had an "Aha!" realization of when she had stopped breathing. It was during a period of heavy emotional stress when she had not wanted to feel the deep emotions she was experiencing. Shortly after this time the depression had settled in, and she had not been able to shake it. I taught her how to do the simple diaphragmatic breathing program described in Foundation Lesson Two, and within minutes she felt better. She continued to practice, and when I checked in with her on the phone the next afternoon, she was feeling back to her normal self again. Not all cases are so quickly resolved, but I have seen many depressions successfully alleviated through breathwork.

Another example involves a more chronic emotional and physical problem. A successful young rock singer I treated had stage fright so severe that it sometimes escalated into an asthma attack. His asthma had been with him since he was in the second grade, and now, as he approached thirty, he was highly motivated to deal with it without medication. He had been prescribed powerful steroids, which were beginning to take their toll on his body. In our breathing work we approached the problem in two ways. First, I helped him learn to breathe through certain core emotions—mainly sadness, fear, and anger—that had plagued him for years. His habit was to hold his breath when his feelings arose, in a misguided attempt to make them go away. By doing this he actually prolonged the

Melancholoke folke are commonly given to sigh, because the minde being possessed by a great varietie and store of foolish apparitions doth not remember or suffer the partie to be at leisure to breathe according to the necessitie of nature.
—DULAURANS, 1559

unpleasant sensation of the feelings. He learned to breathe his way through his emotions instead of holding his breath. At first he found this very difficult, but with practice he learned not to shut down his breathing when in the grip of feeling.

My client discovered something remarkable: When he let himself breathe through the feelings, he was often free of them within seconds. But when he held his breath, the feelings would sometimes linger for hours.

My second intervention was to teach him a specific breathing technique that he could use if he started feeling uncomfortable while onstage. Basically, he learned how to breathe down into his relaxed abdomen. Asthmatics frequently breathe high up in their chests, where there is relatively little blood circulation, so they constantly feel starved for breath. Less than a tenth of a liter of blood flows through the top of the lungs every minute, compared with two-thirds of a liter per minute in the middle. But down at the bottom of the lungs, well over a liter flows through each minute. When my client learned to let his breathing drop into his belly, he felt nurtured by his breath. Now, several years later, he is drug-free and able to control both stage fright and asthma with simple breathing techniques.

The unpleasant qualities of emotions come from not letting them through, from holding on to them by not participating with them. By directly participating with feelings, largely through breathing with them, you can rid yourself of much unnecessary negativity.

CONSCIOUS BREATHING PREVENTS AND HEALS PHYSICAL PROBLEMS

The research literature is full of cases in which healthy breathing principles—usually diaphragmatic breathing—healed physical maladies. I have witnessed dozens of cases of asthma and stress-related disease disappear as people learned effective breathing techniques. The most dramatic case of which I have direct personal knowledge involved a woman who suffered from a rare lung disease that the Stanford School of Medicine had received a grant to study. At that time, in 1989, the researchers had been able to find only a dozen cases of it in the western United States. There was no known cure, although a variety of exotic medicines had been tried.

This client courageously decided to take responsibility for her own healing. She reasoned that since the disease affected her lungs, learning to breathe properly might help. She asked the research team at Stanford to teach her, but no one could tell her what healthy breathing was! Her doctors thought it peculiar that she wanted to learn to breathe. While they did not discourage her, they regarded her effort as a harmless diversion as their search for an effective drug went on. This is not surprising. Many physicians tell me that they are given extensive training in respiratory diseases in medical school, but very little information on how to identify effective breathing, much less how to teach it.

At any rate, the woman found her way to a longtime colleague of mine, Dr. Loic Jassy, and engaged in several sessions of breathwork activities. Within a month the disease disappeared and has not returned. It is a comment on modern medicine that no one in the research project expressed any interest in how she had healed herself. Her cure was entered on the books as a "spontaneous remission."

Today, people are taking charge of their own health. Many have found that simple things—eating healthy foods, exercising, breathing, getting a massage—can have profound health benefits. Western medicine is extremely good at dealing with certain problems such as infections and emergencies. Most people in the grip of a staph infection still choose treatment by antibiotics rather than acupuncture. But with the degenerative diseases Western medicine has a very poor track record.

For example, heart bypass surgery is but the latest in a series of surgical

Nearly every physical problem is accompanied by a disturbance of breathing. But which comes first?
—HANS WELLER, M.D.

interventions, each of which was greeted with great enthusiasm and later found to be of much less value than originally thought. For a thorough discussion of the relative ineffectiveness of bypass surgery, study the remarkable research of Dean Ornish, M.D. His work has demonstrated conclusively that a program of exercise, stress reduction, and a simple vegetarian diet is more effective than surgery at prolonging the life and enhancing the well-being of heart attack patients.

Breathing has a profound relationship to the health of our hearts. When blood pressure was first measured in 1732, Stephen Hales noticed that it rose and fell with the breath. If the person (or the horse, in Hales's case) is breathing normally, the blood pressure will increase slightly with the in-breath and decrease on the out-breath. A tiny structure in the brain called the medulla is responsible for the tone and diameter of the arteries, and the activity of this structure is very sensitive to changes in the quality of the blood circulating through it. Specifically, the medulla reads the amount of carbon dioxide in the blood. If the carbon dioxide/oxygen ratio is imbalanced, the blood pressure is directly affected, usually becoming elevated.

The chest-breather, the pattern that characterizes many heart patients, is chronically in a state of mild hyperventilation, discharging too much carbon dioxide from the blood through short, shallow breaths. This imbalance in the blood causes the heart to work harder, much as a car engine strains and skips when the carburetor is poorly adjusted. For this reason, then, healthy breathing should be the first thing taught to a heart patient. In my office I have seen people with a highly escalated blood pressure, say 180 over 120, return to a normal reading (perhaps 120 over 80) within a one-hour session practicing the lessons given in Part II of this book.

A Dutch study, conducted by a doctor named Dixhoorn, compared two groups of heart attack patients. The first group was taught simple

Improper breathing is a common cause of ill health.
—ANDREW WEIL, M.D.

diaphragmatic breathing, while the second group was given no training in breathing. The breathing group had no further heart attacks, while seven out of the twelve members of the second group had second heart attacks over the next two years.

Another study, done in the coronary care unit of a Minneapolis hospital, examined 153 heart attack patients. The researchers wanted to find out whether these people breathed in the effective abdominal style I will teach you in this book, or in the labored, chest-breathing style caused by having tense abdominal muscles. Astonishingly, the study found that all of the 153 patients were chest-breathers. Not a single one of them breathed in the effective abdominal style. To make things worse, 76 percent of them were mouth-breathers. No wonder their hearts had to work so hard. The Dutch study suggests that a shift to abdominal breathing may nourish the body with oxygen so that the heart does not have to labor excessively to move less-oxygenated blood around the body.

Many healings of other physical troubles have occurred in my clients after they started to integrate breathing practices into their lives. There is a simple but encompassing reason that may explain this. The human body is designed to discharge 70 percent of its toxins through breathing. Only a small percentage of toxins are discharged through sweat, defecation, and urination. If your breathing is not operating at peak efficiency, you are not ridding yourself of toxins properly. If less than 70 percent of your toxins are being released through breathing, other systems of your body, such as your kidneys, must work overtime. This overwork can set the stage for a number of illnesses.

Nowhere can this phenomenon be observed more immediately than on the skin. The skin is a direct beneficiary of better breathing. In workshops over the years I have always brought to people's attention the healthy changes in their skin color as the breathwork progresses. The skin

A significant number of people who think they have serious heart disease are almost certainly actually suffering from breathing disorders.
—SHELDON SAUL HENDLER, M.D.

is the body's largest organ, and when you breathe effectively, you send more health-giving oxygen to it. Few people realize that the skin is an organ that helps in the elimination of toxins from the body. If the breathing mechanism is not doing its job, the skin must take over some of the responsibility. When you learn to breathe well, you use the full potential of your lungs, which frees the skin from overwork. It will celebrate its new-found freedom by looking better.

CONSCIOUS BREATHING CONTRIBUTES TO GRACEFUL AGING

The ability to breathe deeply is supposed to decline with age, but at the Hendricks Institute we have collected a considerable amount of data that disputes this supposed truism. We use a simple machine called a Voldyne, which measures the amount of breathing capacity on the in-breath. Placing a tube in your mouth, you inhale through the machine, and it gives you a number that indicates your vital capacity. When I began testing myself ten years ago, I was at the normal number for my age. Now, after ten years of practicing the program in this book, I have the breathing capacity of a six-foot-six nineteen-year-old, according to the chart that accompanies the Voldyne. We have found that people "youth" themselves in breathing capacity, often within the first session. I have shared the delight of my clients on dozens of occasions as they have improved their Voldyne scores after a half-hour of conscious breathing practice.

I had not given much thought to the usefulness of conscious breathing in the aging process until the mother of a friend and colleague, Richard Beyer, came to one of our breathing workshops in 1981. She introduced herself to me by saying, "I'm Fawnie Beyer and I'm here at seventy-seven years old to learn how to breathe." She turned out to be a delightful person, and I checked on her periodically throughout the day to make sure she was doing well with the activities. I spotted her main breathing problems right away—she was a chest-breather, and she held her breath at the top of the inhalation—and showed her how to correct them. The change in her energy level from just that one intervention was amazing. Her cheeks brightened, and as the day went on, she got visibly stronger. After the workshop, she sent me a card from time to time, telling me that she was still practicing her breathing. At this writing she continues in good health, now in her tenth decade.

This positive initial experience caused me to review the research literature on breathing and aging. There was not much at the time, and there still isn't now, although there is some movement in that direction. My own clinical research has proven to my satisfaction that conscious breathing is very useful to older adults. I have worked now with about sixty people in the sixty-five-and-older category, teaching them the breathing program described in this book. The combination of breathing and movement is particularly helpful in aging. Joint pain is probably the most common complaint of aging adults. When you link up diaphragmatic breathing with slow, gentle movements, you have a very healthful combination. Most of the activities in the book feature this combination.

Your breathing determines whether you are at your best or whether you are at a disadvantage.
—CAROLA H. SPEADS

CONSCIOUS BREATHING MANAGES PAIN

Pain can be reduced, even eliminated, through conscious breathing activities. In fact, most people today are first introduced to breathing techniques through the exercises taught in natural childbirth classes. I have had the opportunity to serve as a breathing coach for many women during pregnancy and birth. In a recent birth that my wife and I attended, the laboring woman used her breath to breathe into the contractions, participating with the sensations rather than fighting them. By doing so, she was able to transform the pain. Later, she said that it was never painful while she was using her breath. Sometimes a contraction would start as pain, but as she remembered to breathe into it, a shift would occur: Pain would become sensation.

Conscious breathing can be used for both chronic and acute pain. Let me first give a typical example of the alleviation of chronic pain through breathwork, then follow with an example of acute pain.

Back pain is the most common chronic pain syndrome in the United States. I was consulted by a business executive for a problem unrelated to back pain. He was going through the troublesome aftermath of a divorce, with fluctuations of mood and emotion. He mentioned back pain as an afterthought, telling me that he had suffered from it since college. Wincing as he sat down and got up, he said that it had gotten worse after the divorce. As we talked, I noticed that he had almost no movement in his belly as he breathed, and that his stiff posture allowed no flexing of his spine with the breath.

I demonstrated the first three Advanced Lessons, lying down on the floor myself, then I taught them to him. He felt some immediate relief, but over the next week what he later called "a real miracle" occurred. Practicing the activities no more than fifteen minutes twice a day, he was completely pain-free by our next session! The simple act of reestablishing the correct flow to his breath and movement allowed him to clear up a problem that had bothered him for twenty years.

My own most dramatic use of conscious breathing to manage acute pain has come relatively recently: I have started using breathing instead of anesthesia to have my teeth drilled and filled. In 1993 I had my annual dental check-up, and to my chagrin my dentist found a cavity. I am a zealous flosser and brusher, so this came as a surprise to me. My dentist told me it might be due to a composite filling simply wearing out. Composite apparently does not wear as well as metal or porcelain.

When the dentist came in, he said, "Are you ready?"

I said yes, and he asked for his Novocain needle.

"Hold on, Don," I said. "Don't you remember? I'm the guy who doesn't use anesthetic."

He glanced at his notes. "Oh, yes," he said. "You do some sort of self-hypnosis, don't you?"

"Sort of," I said. "But it's really a lot simpler than that. I just do slow, connected breathing and try to keep from holding my breath."

"Well, then," he said, reaching for his drill. "Let's do it."

I have found that I can manage any discomfort in the dental chair with conscious breathing. I have not tried it out on anything complicated like a root canal or periodontal surgery, but for routine work I have not used anesthesia in recent years. The director of our institute, Kathy Allen, used the technique for a long root canal procedure, with the same positive results.

The trick is this: Take slow, deep breaths, and notice when you hold your breath. I focus my mind on the here-and-now, zeroing my attention in on the sounds and sensations of the moment. In other words, I don't try to visualize myself at the beach or in a wooded glen while I'm in the dental chair. I simply try to be there as much as I can. The sensations of the drill biting into the tooth, the occasional twinge of pain, the bouncy Muzak in the background—these are the things I focus on. As Henry Kissinger once said in a different context, "An absence of alternatives clears the mind marvelously."

When Don fired up the drill, I involuntarily held my breath. This is a major problem in dealing with pain. There is a universal tendency to hold our breath when we feel pain. We think perhaps we can control sensation

Breathing in, I calm body and mind.
Breathing out, I smile.
Dwelling in the present moment,
I know this is the only moment.
— THICH NHAT HANH

by stopping the breath. There is some truth to this, but of course it is a short-term solution. Eventually we must breathe and face the pain. The second problem is that it is not simply pain that causes us to hold our breath. It is the anticipation of pain. There is nothing intrinsically painful about the sound of a dental drill, but it symbolizes a world of hurt for many of us.

I had plenty of personal reasons for going into fight-or-flight breathing at the sound of a dental drill. I grew up in the swamplands of central Florida and did not get on speaking terms with a toothbrush until I was a teenager. By then, my mouth was riddled with cavities, from neglect and from the standard southern fare of pecan pie, moon pies, soft drinks, and chewing gum. No southern youngster can be long without a big wad of gum in the mouth, and it takes its toll. When my family got out of poverty in my teens, I spent much time in the dental chair, getting the damage repaired. My dentist back then was a big, angry man who wielded his drill and pick with a vengeance. I dreaded my visits to him, because I knew there would be no sympathy from this hulking, red-faced fundamentalist who saw cavities as an affront to the Lord and dentistry as his way of striking back at the work of the Devil.

So it wasn't surprising that I clutched my breath when Don's drill began to whine. A second later, I realized what I was doing and forced myself to take a deep, slow breath. For the next half-hour I continued in this way. I breathed deeply and consciously, focusing my mind on the sensations in my body—the breath flowing in and out, the pains and vibrations in my mouth—and on the sounds and sights around me. Occasionally I lost awareness of the breath. My mind would wander, or I would catch myself holding my breath. When I noticed what I was doing, I would return to the breath—slow, steady, connected. On two occasions the pain got fairly intense. This feeling inspired me to focus on my breath with equal intensity. Before I knew it, Don was finished. I got up, thanked him, and left. A half-hour later I was having lunch in my favorite restaurant, with none of the bothersome aftereffects of Novocain.

CONSCIOUS BREATHING ENHANCES MENTAL CONCENTRATION AND PHYSICAL PERFORMANCE

Learning to use your breath to get through difficult experiences is important, but breathing can also be used to help you express your positive potential. Athletic performance is a direct beneficiary. A middle-aged runner visited me to work with his breathing the day before an important 10-kilometer race. His typical time for this length of race was around fifty-four minutes. I watched him breathe for a couple of minutes as he ran on a treadmill. I noticed he was tensing slightly on his in-breath. Although subtle, this habit was keeping him from getting a full breath into his lungs. Using video to help him see his pattern, he made a tiny adjustment and immediately felt the difference. The next day he shaved nearly a minute off his best time. The most dramatic improvement I have yet seen was with a woman marathon runner who dropped thirty minutes from her usual four-hour time after one lesson.

When I remember to breathe, my serve goes in. When I don't, it doesn't.
—BILL TILDEN

You may wonder, if breathing is so therapeutic, why athletes, joggers, and aerobic dancers are not completely enlightened beings. With all that breath flooding their systems, shouldn't they be uniformly happy and healthy? There is no denying that physical exercise is healthful, but exercise burns up the oxygen as soon as it comes in. The energy does not get down into the deeper parts of ourselves that breathwork is designed to nourish. In breathwork, you are being still and allowing the energy generated by the oxygen to penetrate to those parts of you most in need of it.

I live in Colorado Springs, home of the Olympic Training Center, and this has given me the opportunity to observe and fine-tune the breathing of a number of top athletes. One fascinating fact I've learned is that many fine athletes have breathing problems. I have worked with at least a dozen cyclists and runners who were asthmatic as children or who still suffer from difficulties with their breathing. The techniques in this book work extremely well in enhancing athletic performance. Regardless of the sport, I have yet to find an athlete who could not make some improvement in performance through this program.

The number-one problem I have had to correct in athletes is the over-reliance on chest-breathing during exertion. One of my own enthusiasms is cycling. My wife and I have ridden our bikes on four continents, and we have published three bicycle-tour guidebooks. So I have had considerable experience learning to breathe correctly as I ride. Over the past ten years I have spent upward of a thousand hours observing and correcting the breathing of cyclists practicing on exercise bicycles. This sport is difficult for a breathing coach, because the rider is often stretched out over the bike instead of upright. In addition, it is one of the most physically challenging of all sports. In spite of these difficulties, much improvement is possible when riders learn to open up their breathing downward into their bellies. There is a "magic moment" when they discover how to breathe in both belly and chest during exertion. The moment the breath deepens, speed and endurance go up.

Mental concentration also improves with healthy breathing. Although I did not have a context to put it in, I actually made my first discovery in this area when I was just entering high school. One night I was working on my algebra homework when I noticed I was holding my breath. I also saw that I had a death-grip on my pencil. I found myself wondering: Why all the tension? What is there about algebra that's got me so worked up? In a flood of insight, I realized that I was afraid I wouldn't live up to my older brother. He was a superstar in high school, and I was about to go through four years of having the same teachers whose faces he had so

What are my chances when they load the bases with nobody out? I never doubt myself. I just step back, take a deep breath, and figure out what I have to do.
—DWIGHT GOODEN

thoroughly lit up. Math was his strong suit, but it definitely wasn't mine. It was a moment of accepting that I was never going to be my brother, so I had better be me. I don't recall noticing what happened to my breathing, but I clearly remember loosening my white-knuckle grip on the pencil.

Anyone who needs long periods of mental focus would do well to practice conscious breathing. The best way I have found to refresh the mind is to take deep, slow breaths when attention drifts. When concentrating, there is a tendency to move the body less. The decreased movement brings in less oxygen, and the brain is oxygen's biggest customer. If you can remember to take deep breaths now and then, and move your body around a little, your periods of mental concentration will often be longer and easier.

CONSCIOUS BREATHING FACILITATES PSYCHOSPIRITUAL TRANSFORMATION

There are several ways that conscious breathing can facilitate processes of personal growth. One that I see every week is the power of conscious breathing to dissolve limiting programs that are stored in the mind and body. One of the great wake-up moments of my professional life was discovering the work of the great Canadian neurologist Wilder Penfield. Although he made many discoveries, the one that changed my worldview involved his experiments in stimulating various places on the surface of patients' brains. He would place an electrode in a specific place and send a tiny amount of electricity into the spot. When this occurred, the patient would have a specific memory of an event. He even found a place in the brain that seemed to be the reminiscence zone. When he stimulated it, people reliably would reminisce!

This discovery proved to my satisfaction that we store our histories in

You can use conscious breathing and willingness in each and every moment to balance your energy, face a challenge, love yourself and others, and release your creativity.
—SUJATA

our minds. But a second discovery was even more remarkable. In the early seventies I made the acquaintance of Ida Rolf and some of her trainees. She was the inventor of a form of deep body massage—variously called Structural Integration or Rolfing—that produces lasting structural changes in the body. After witnessing one demonstration, I signed up for it myself. Rolf would work on a particular part of a person's body, perhaps the chest, and the person would relive specific events. What seemed to be occurring was that the tissue-memory of the event was being released into the mind and the physical restrictions were being cleared out. This showed me that our histories were written in our bodies as well as in our minds.

Later when I was Rolfed, the fourth session worked on my legs. It was particularly painful, but at the peak of the pain a memory appeared full-blown in my mind. I relived an injury playing high school football. But there were more layers to the memory, including the reason I was playing football: to get the love and approval of my grandfather and my father. I had never realized why I was so intent on playing football, especially in light of my negligible athletic skills. Suddenly, the information appeared fourteen years after the fact, under a set of skilled probing fingers.

Similar events occur in conscious breathing. As they learn breathwork, many clients encounter early life events and clear away deeply held beliefs about life. For example, they may uncover an "I'm not good enough" or an "I'm not wanted here" belief that has been buried in their body perhaps from their first day on earth. As you learn to breathe consciously, you oxygenate whatever area of your bodymind needs it. As I have said, people hold their breath when they are hurt; this is a normal human reaction. But if this pattern is repeated, it becomes programmed into the body. Later as you breathe consciously, you can free yourself from these limits.

The first session of breathwork I did with a client after moving to Colorado illustrates the limit-releasing potential of breathing. A young real estate salesman was coping with his wife's attraction to another man. He was feeling a great deal of anxiety and had been sleepless for several nights. I asked him to breathe with the fear, amplifying it rather than trying to control it. He went through a powerful reaction of shudders followed by sobbing. At the end of this catharsis, which took about twenty minutes, he spontaneously realized that he had been paralyzed by the fear, which reminded him of the death of his mother in childhood. After he had breathed through the fear, he found that he was able to talk to his wife in a straightforward way, asking for and getting an agreement that she would have no physical contact with the man.

Another example of the release of a limiting program comes from a thirty-seven-year-old businesswoman: "As I was doing the breathing activity, I began to feel new energy flowing through my body. This energy brought with it a sense of love. Once I felt this natural love flowing through me, a thought popped into my mind—'I am willing to do whatever I need to do to feel this love in my life all the time.' I then started thinking of my money problems. It occurred to me that I had been stopping myself from having all the money I needed because I thought money would keep me separate from my spiritual growth. I suddenly realized that I could have money and have a commitment to the development of my spirituality. This idea brought me a huge wave of release. Afterward I had a surge of new ideas on how I could make my work more prosperous."

Conscious breathing activities also increase our ability to handle more energy. Many of us have our positive-energy thermostat set very low, so that we do not allow ourselves as much pleasure as we could. Conscious breathing actually retrains your nervous system to tolerate a higher charge of energy, and if you practice it with any sort of regularity, you will find

There is one way of breathing that is shameful and constricted. Then there's another way: a breath of love that takes you all the way to infinity.
—RUMI

that you can expand your ability to feel good past your previous limits. If you practice these breathing activities for a while, you may have very deep experiences of positive energy. After practicing breathwork for a few months, one person reported a particularly deep session: "I felt like I was plugged into a universal light socket. My body felt illuminated from within. I felt orgasmic rushes every time I took a deep breath."

Sometimes when you are doing the breathing activities, you will run up against a particularly tense place in your body. One man reported, "As I breathed, I felt like the energy was getting stuck in my hands and arms. I couldn't figure out how to let it go. This happened for several sessions in a row. This may sound strange, but I finally asked my arms what they needed in order to let go. A few seconds later, I had the urge to reach out with my arms, even though I was sitting alone in my bedroom. Suddenly I was flooded with tears, and I had the realization of how much I hold back from reaching out to people. Immediately the tension melted and never returned in subsequent sessions."

In the practice of conscious breathing, you also have the opportunity to look at and deal with the problem of resistance. Many therapists think that resistance is the key psychological problem we must learn to handle. For example, it is not our feelings that bother most of us, it is our resistance to those feelings. If you allow yourself to feel sad and cry, the sadness is usually experienced and released quickly. If you resist feeling sad and crying, perhaps out of a belief that "big boys/girls don't cry," you may carry that feeling with you for decades. The same is true for positive feelings. It is not a lack of love that troubles most of us; it is our resistance to the love all around us.

Probably two-thirds of a therapist's time is spent helping people contact, acknowledge, and express feelings that have been resisted for a long time. Hence, a standard therapy aphorism is "What you resist persists."

Breathing can be one of the fastest ways to get past resistance. The reason is that resistance exists on the borderline between the unconscious and the conscious. So does breathing. It is the one system in your body that you can control with your conscious mind or that you can forget about completely, leaving it to be run by your unconscious. No other body system is so exquisitely sensitive to your will.

One client described her experience this way: "During breathing one day I found myself getting bored. I felt sleepy and thought, 'This stuff is really stupid.' Suddenly I realized that the feelings and thoughts were just resistance. I remembered what someone told me once, that resistance is a sign that a breakthrough is about to happen. So I kept on breathing, and I became aware of a tense place deep in my stomach. I breathed into it for just a few breaths, and the tension burst free like an exploding sun. I was filled with light. I had the realization that I had lived my whole life like a robot, never thinking of what I wanted or needed. Doing this had put a ball of tension in my stomach that had been there for years." Through working with her breath, she learned to let go of this ball of tension.

Breathwork in its deeper forms can help you breathe free of limiting patterns laid down in infancy, birth, and your first moments as a conceived being. Here we are moving into territory that is difficult to prove in the scientific sense but that I have seen clinically many times. After an extended period of breathing, clients often have memories of birth and even earlier events such as conception. Breathing affects every cell in your body, and there is mounting evidence that the cells themselves contain imprints of past events. When you breathe deeply enough, you are likely to stimulate a form of cellular memory that can aid you in the resolution of early trauma. During therapy I often ask a client to breathe into a problem feeling. As the session goes along, the person may sense that the feeling actually goes back to birth itself. Sometimes it is not even the client's own

Deep, flowing breath is essentially arousing and exciting.
—Michael Sky

feeling but belongs to the mother, the father, or someone else in the environment. These moments are often of great therapeutic importance, because the person is contacting and breathing through the feeling at its source.

Here is how one person experienced the healing of a birth issue: "I had been doing the breathwork for over a year when one day an energy vibration began happening in my chest. It felt like a light radiating out through my arms. Suddenly a memory flashed into my mind of being a baby lying on a cold surface. My mother was there, but something was wrong with her, and she was the focus of attention. I felt very cold and very sad. I'm adopted so I don't know how to check any of this out, but it seemed very real. Afterward I cried some during the breathing and ended the session feeling light and calm."

I have seen many people have spontaneous experiences of love, forgiveness, and joy while doing breathwork. These feelings are all the more important because they have emerged from the body rather than from the mind. For example, many people have reported that, while they had previously *understood* the concept of forgiveness, it was only during breathwork that they actually *experienced* it internally. It is much more valuable to have a felt experience of a positive emotion than only the mental idea of it.

I have also seen people breathe their way to a sense of unity with themselves, others, and the universe itself. Deep spiritual experiences like these have great healing potential because they put the person in touch with a power greater than their normal ego consciousness. Although I have meditated for years and practiced many other spiritual disciplines, I can attest that breathwork has been the source of some of my deepest spiritual experiences.

The highest potential of breathing is in unifying mind, body, and spirit. When people feel integrated, they feel good. While good breathing can prevent many health problems, the main benefit I have found for these

And now I see with eye serene,
the very pulse of the machine.
A being breathing thoughtful breath,
A traveler between life and death.
—WILLIAM WORDSWORTH

techniques is in helping healthy people feel even better. There is no upper limit to how good you can feel. Once you learn that good feelings are only a few breaths away, you have a skill you can use for life. Once you clear out major distortions in your breathing, you can turn your attention to using your breath to raise your positive energy thermostat each day.

Breath has infinite subtleties that can keep the keenest student of phenomenology busy for a lifetime. I have been working with my own breathing now for almost two decades, yet not a day goes by that I do not make a noticeable improvement in my breathing. It is a very rich subject, and one with an unusual potential: the more you learn, the better you feel. No wonder, then, that all the major spiritual traditions of the world have made use of breathing activities to enrich their faiths.

Ultimately, breathing can be a path to that most essential of human experiences: learning to love. Almost everyone who begins to work with their breathing finds that it is an essential helpmate in their quest to love themselves and others more perfectly. Your breathing will help you feel and clear the barriers to loving yourself, and it will show you where you are holding back in giving and receiving love with others. The spiritual potential of conscious breathing is beautifully expressed in one of the beatitudes of Jesus. Contemporary scholar Neal Douglas Klotz has written a book, *Prayers of the Cosmos,* in which he renders the beatitudes in the original Aramaic language spoken by Jesus. The familiar translation says, "Blessed are the poor in spirit." But in the original Aramaic language the beatitude had a very different meaning: "Happy and aligned with the One are those who find their home in the breathing."

We are children of breath, and the way is ever open for our return to a life divine and everlasting.
—MICHAEL SKY

CHAPTER 2

How I Use Conscious Breathing Every Day

To give you a deeper sense of conscious breathing, I would like to describe how I use it during a typical day. You will see how the practice of conscious breathing can be integrated into the sometimes ho-hum details of life, to make each moment rich with the possibilities of transformation. Then I will take you into my office to show you how my professional practice of conscious breathing looks and feels.

Let me start with a quick and simple demonstration. Right now it is a little after three o'clock in the afternoon, and I have been working since nine this morning. I can feel the edges of fatigue beginning to form in my body. I wouldn't say I'm actually tired yet, but I can sense the beginnings of it. As I tune in to my body, I realize that I feel the fatigue in several places. There is a line of tiredness across my abdomen. Am I holding my stomach muscles too tightly? Perhaps. I take a deep breath into the area of

Your shoulder muscles can restrict your breathing. Your chest muscles can restrict your breathing. Your ankle muscles can restrict your breathing.
—Michael Grant White

tension and let the breath go with a sigh. Immediately the fatigue disappears and is replaced by a warm and streaming sensation of energy. I pause and listen to my body. I can feel the fatigue coming back, maybe a little fainter but still there. I relax my stomach and take another big breath, slowly filling my lungs to their capacity, then let the air go. This time I listen to my body for a minute or so, and the tired feeling seems to have gone away. This is conscious breathing at its simplest.

Here are some experiences of conscious breathing from yesterday. My wife, Kathlyn, and I got up around six-thirty, chatted for a few minutes over a cup of coffee, then went into my study to do some breathing and stretching. My study has a large expanse of comfortable carpeting, so we tend to use it for our morning routine. I turned on National Public Radio's *Morning Edition* and lay down. I first did about twenty deep, slow breaths, using the process described in Foundation Lesson Two. I lay on my back, bringing my knees up so that my feet were flat on the floor. As I breathed deeply into my belly, I arched the small of my back gently. As I breathed slowly out, I flattened my lower back against the floor. This arching and flattening of the lower back gives my whole spine a good morning stretch.

Since I have been starting every day this way, I have not had any back pain. This is remarkable to me, because I had a lot of back problems in my twenties and early thirties. Then, in my midthirties I began doing a few minutes of breathing and stretching every day, and the problems disappeared. Now I'm in my late forties, with a decade or so of pain-free flexibility under my belt. When I finished twenty breaths, I stretched my legs out for a moment and enjoyed the streaming feeling of ease coursing through my whole body.

Next, I did two of the Advanced Lessons, stretching all the joints of my body as I continued to take full, slow breaths. The whole set of activities took me a little less than ten minutes. When I finished I felt clear, alert, and limber.

Next, I settled into my easy chair to get ready for meditation. Kathlyn and I are both longtime meditators, and unless we are traveling apart from each other, we always meditate together. We find it a great boon to our relationship to sit quietly in each other's presence while we meditate. After studying Zen, Vipassana, and a couple of other forms of meditation, I learned Transcendental Meditation twenty years ago, when I was in graduate school. I found it much more beneficial than any other form I had practiced, so I made it a part of my daily routine. Twenty years later I am infinitely grateful for it. The benefits of meditation in my life could fill a separate book. Suffice it to say that it blends beautifully with the body-centered therapy that we practice and with the breathing and movement activities that we do ourselves.

As I rested in my chair, I practiced the alternate-nostril breathing described in Foundation Lesson Three. I find that it sharpens my mind as well as relaxes me in preparation for meditation. After about five minutes of alternate-nostril breathing, my mind felt clear and filled with light. I eased into my mantra and began meditation, finishing forty-five minutes later feeling blissfully expanded. Then I went down to the kitchen and helped Kathlyn make some fresh apple juice. I took a big glass of fresh juice up to my writing room and worked on this book for a couple of hours. I usually devote the first part of my morning to writing, before I do any other kind of work like seeing clients or taking care of paperwork.

While sitting at my computer, I took many conscious breaths. I have learned to use certain body-cues as reminders to take a conscious breath or two. One cue is a slightly achy feeling in my back, shoulders, and arms that is a signal to me that I'm getting tired. As I typed, I seemed to feel this cue every five or ten minutes. Whenever I felt it, I would take a few

Without full awareness of breathing, there can be no development of meditative stability and understanding.
—THICH NHAT HANH

deep belly-breaths and change my body position slightly. The achy feeling would immediately disappear. After a couple of hours of writing, I was finished for the morning.

The next time I recall using conscious breathing was on an errand-run late in the morning. I was heading downtown to buy a couple of things when I got stopped by a traffic snarl. A traffic jam is an unusual event in Colorado Springs. (In fact, the ease of getting around is one of the reasons I love living here.) I felt a prickle of irritation creep over me as I sat in my car. After a few hostile snorts, I realized I was holding my breath and getting angry. I acknowledged the anger and remembered to breathe again, switching to deep, slow belly-breaths. Within a few breaths my irritation had completely smoothed out, and I felt relaxed and happy again. The feeling I like to maintain in my body is a streaming, breezelike sensation in my belly and chest. I call it *flow*. I take care to notice when I am out of flow. Usually it is because of some emotion I am withholding. A few good breaths are usually all it takes to reestablish flow in my body. I got back to flow as I sat in my car, and about ten seconds later the traffic started to flow, too.

In line at the post office I encountered another slowdown, and I found myself mentally prescribing Prozac and double espressos for the clerks. I remembered to take a few conscious breaths, and my cynical thoughts shifted up the emotional tone-scale toward compassion. I enjoyed using the minute or two I was in line as a breathing practice. Later, on the golf course, I used a similar technique to steady myself. (I'll pass it along to golfers everywhere in Chapter 10.)

I don't recall doing anything else with my breathing until I saw my first therapy client of the day. George was in a great deal of physical and emotional pain. Many times during the session I noticed that I was holding my breath, probably in a misguided attempt to help him hurt less. Each time I noticed I was holding my breath, he seemed to be holding his, too. When I remembered to breathe, so would he. George had learned something early in life that was causing him a great deal of trouble. His parents were both busy doctors who were not very approachable on the emotional level. So George learned to get sick when he was in emotional pain. Physical illness guaranteed a rapid infusion of attention from his parents. By middle age, George's pattern of substituting physical pain for emotional contact had caused him to injure his lower back, so that practically every movement he made hurt him. Wisely, he had decided to handle some of the emotions that were the undercurrent of his life, in the hope that he could break the pattern of physical pain.

Hidden anger is often the culprit in low back pain, and it turned out to be so in George's case. Two tasks confronted me as a therapist. One, I needed to help George learn to handle anger more effectively. Learning to deal with anger is a two-step process. The first step is learning to acknowledge it to yourself, so that you know you're angry when you're angry. There are formidable obstacles to this level of self-knowledge, because many of us have built a lifestyle around denying our feelings to ourselves. For people with chronic pain, acknowledging feelings to themselves is a crucial step. I have found that it is the act of hiding their feelings from themselves that contributes to their pain. The second step is to learn how to communicate anger in a straightforward way to other people. There is an old saying in therapy circles to the effect that "You don't need therapy anymore when you can talk about your sexual feelings, your anger, and your death without flinching." George was far from this level, but he was on the track.

More urgently, I wanted to assist him in hurting less. Conscious breathing came into play in both tasks. I started with the biggest problem first, and that was his physical pain. I invited George to lie down on a mat on the floor. Using a very slowed-down form of Foundation Lesson Two,

It is certainly not the aim of breathing work, nor is it possible, to have one's breathing unaffected by life or to avoid life's problems. On the contrary, contact with your breathing will make you more open to life's experiences.
—CAROLA H. SPEADS

I asked him to breathe in and out of his relaxed belly, while at the same time arching and flattening his lower back gently. We worked together until he was taking a very slow breath. By slowing down the breath and the movement of the spine, he found that he could move his back without pain. As long as he breathed very consciously and coordinated his movement with his breath, there was no pain. When he "lost it" and sped up the movement or when he forgot to stay with his breathing, the pain would return. This was a powerful motivation to be very conscious about his movements and his breath.

We kept up this activity for about fifteen minutes, until a relaxed smile replaced the grimace that had been on his face when he came in. While he was relaxed, I talked to him about anger. I told him that he needed to be with his anger in a new way. Instead of hiding it in his body and pretending his anger did not exist, he needed to learn to express it clearly in a straightforward way. This idea made the relaxed smile disappear from his face; he had a flurry of reasons why he could not possibly communicate his anger to others. They couldn't handle it, they wouldn't like him, it wasn't safe, he didn't know how. I invited him to notice that those were just thoughts and to go back to his slow breathing.

This time it only took a dozen or so conscious breaths to put the smile back on his face. "I think I'm beginning to get it," he said. "When I hide anger, I stop breathing. Then I hurt. When I breathe and acknowledge my anger, the pain goes away."

"Well said," I told him. "You'll notice dozens of times a day when you stuff little flickers of anger. Now when you can remember to acknowledge and breathe through them, you'll notice the pain fades."

I helped him go through a few more cycles of losing the breath and getting it back again. We scheduled an appointment for the following week, and I saw him to the door.

Next, I zipped up the freeway to give a lecture. The scene: An auditorium where I am about to conduct a demonstration of breathwork for several hundred psychotherapists and medical doctors. I ask for a volunteer from the audience, specifying that I would like someone who had some stress symptom he or she would like to clear up. Stress symptoms are common annoyances to most of us, and they respond very well to conscious breathing exercises. A gentleman raises his hand and says he feels tired and has a slight headache. I invite him to the front, and he sits down in a straight-backed chair brought in from a neighboring classroom. After learning his name, Dan, and asking him if he has any known medical problems that might be contributing to his fatigue or pain (he doesn't), I take a look at his breathing.

At a glance the problem is clear. Like many people, he is breathing upside down. In healthy breathing the stomach muscles are relaxed, allowing the breath to swell the abdomen with each breath. In upside-down breathing, the stomach muscles are tight and the breath inflates the chest. Dan's breathing is largely up in his chest. His stomach muscles are very tight, preventing movement in his belly. If the abdominal muscles are too tight, the diaphragm (the main muscle involved in breathing) cannot move through its full range of motion. As a result, Dan's breathing is shallow and more rapid than is healthy. Using the exact techniques you will learn in this book, I coach Dan for about fifteen minutes. At about the ten-minute mark, we successfully get his breathing right-side up, and he breaks into a smile. There is no need to explain that to the audience. They reward it with a round of applause.

At the end of the fifteen minutes, I ask Dan whether he feels tired or headachy. "No," he says, "I feel great." He goes back to his seat, and I conclude the lecture. Afterward, a medical doctor comes up front to talk with me. He asks me a question I've never before been asked: "How did

Shallow breathers poison themselves.
—PAUL BRAGG

you have the confidence that this was going to work? What if nothing had happened?" I realize that twenty years of breathwork has given me such confidence that whether it would work or not had never entered my mind! "It always works," I hear myself telling him. "It just doesn't fail."

It is this confidence in the power of breathing that I wish for you to develop as we proceed together.

PART II

The Practice of Conscious Breathing

Three Foundation Lessons in Conscious Breathing

T̲O BEGIN, I WOULD LIKE TO SHOW YOU the three foundation practices that I teach to nearly everyone with whom I work. Even if you have been a longtime student of the breath, I think you will find great value in these three fundamental explorations. If you are a newcomer to conscious breathing, you may find, as many of my clients have, that these practices can actually be lifesavers.

Genius is the ability to reduce the complicated to the simple.
—C. W. CERAN

In the first lesson you will explore your breathing, and the physical mechanisms that govern it, from the inside out. Think of it as an experiential anatomy lesson of the most practical sort. In the second lesson you put this awareness into practice by learning how to take a full, deep diaphragmatic breath, just as nature intended. In the third lesson we explore alternate-nostril breathing, a quick, simple, and powerful application of conscious breathing. With this foundation, we will then move on to the Advanced Lessons.

MASTERING THE UNIVERSAL PROBLEM OF BREATHING

As you have probably gathered by now, if there is one universal breathing problem, it is poor diaphragmatic breathing. People tense their bellies as they breathe so that the diaphragm does not move freely with the breath. This problem has a very powerful impact on the breath, for a very fundamental reason.

Human beings have been walking upright for quite a while now, and the fact of gravity has fashioned a quirk of physiology. At the top of your lungs, up near your collarbones, the rate of blood flow is less than a tenth of a liter per minute. In other words, only a half-teacup or so of blood moves through the upper part of your lungs every minute. By contrast, the blood flow at the bottom of your lungs, down toward the bottom of your rib cage, is well over a liter per minute. Most of the blood circulation is in the bottom third of the lungs. If your belly muscles are tense, preventing you from breathing deeply into your abdomen, you are not getting the oxygen down to where all the blood is. This is why if you corrected only this one problem and did nothing else, you would make major improvements in your mental, emotional, and physical functioning. We will use correct diaphragmatic breathing as the jumping-off place for all the activities that follow.

If you want to see healthy diaphragmatic breathing, watch the way a baby breathes. The belly rises and falls effortlessly with the breath. The chest moves somewhat, but the primary movement is below the diaphragm. Later, breathing becomes restricted as the baby is affected by the various shocks life has to offer. It is rare to see poor diaphragmatic breathing in kindergarten, but it is rare to find proper diaphragmatic breathing by high school.

When you establish correct diaphragmatic breathing, your breath rate

I strongly suspect that all children engage in "advanced" breathing/healing practices, only to forget them as the habits of age literally take the breath away.
—MICHAEL SKY

will usually drop from 14 to 15 breaths per minute to 8 to 12 breaths per minute. This is because you are getting more deeply oxygenated so that your lungs don't have to work as hard. Your heart rate will slow also, because it does not have to pump as much blood to get a full supply of oxygen to the body.

The diaphragm is a crucial element in health. It is located between the bottom of the lungs and the top of the abdomen. As you can see in Figure 1, the diaphragm is shaped like a dome. It is a thin sheet of very strong muscle fiber, extending from front to back and side to side. Just above it are the lungs, while just below it are the vital organs of the abdominal cavity. A good way to visualize the diaphragm is to think of a drumhead. If your abdominal cavity were a snare drum, its playing surface, loosened considerably, would be your diaphragm.

When you breathe in, this dome flattens. Assuming your belly muscles are relaxed, your abdomen will expand with the in-breath. If your belly muscles are tight, you will not be able to get a full breath into the bottom of your lungs, your diaphragm will not flatten completely, and your abdomen will not expand. Nature has designed your breathing so that it will make your abdomen expand with each in-breath. As this expansion occurs, the vital organs get room to move and circulation occurs more freely. Nature, then, has wired in a massage for the organs on each breath. But all of this hinges on correct diaphragmatic breathing, without which the massage does not occur. According to one medical researcher, poor breathing plays a role in more than 75 percent of the ills people bring to their doctors. In most cases, poor diaphragmatic breathing is the culprit.

On the good news side, this problem can be significantly reduced very quickly. In fact, I have not seen anybody fail to learn diaphragmatic breathing when given the instructions that follow. You can do all the breathing activities in this book in several ways. You can simply read the

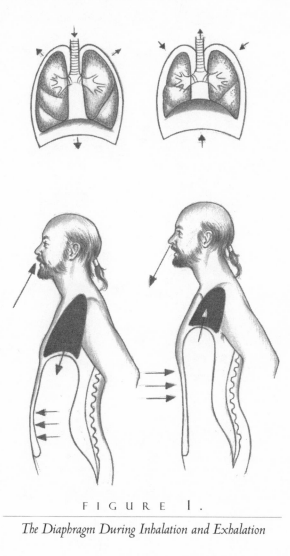

FIGURE 1.

The Diaphragm During Inhalation and Exhalation

instructions to yourself and then carry them out. However, some people find they learn better when someone else reads the instructions to them as they practice. Others record the instructions on tape so that they can be played back later.

Throughout this book I have done my best to write the instructions just as I give them in actual sessions. If you prefer to listen to and watch the instructions, you can order a videotape from the address given in Appendix C. However you go about doing these lessons, do them slowly, mindfully, and with patience. With practice you may come to feel, as I do, that conscious breathing is the pinnacle of the mind/body connection.

All the breathing lessons in this book are designed to be done in the comfort zone. You are never to breathe effortfully. In fact, just the opposite is true. Do the activities very gently, very slowly, with conscious attention. If you perform them correctly, you will discover how easy breathing can be.

The main way you could do these exercises wrong would be to try too hard. There are several symptoms that will let you know you are performing them wrong. If you get dizzy, tense, or uncomfortable in any way, you are doing the activity wrong. If you feel any of these symptoms, immediately pause and rest, resuming the activity only when you can do it more gently.

Always be sure to check with your health care professional before starting any new regimen. This is doubly important if you are in treatment for any breathing problems or any diseases, such as diabetes, in which breathing problems are a secondary symptom. If you are asthmatic or experience other respiratory dysfunction, conscious breathing could be the best thing in the world for you. The processes in this book have been helpful to thousands of people with breathing problems. Just be sure you get your doctor's support for this or any other breathing program. Asthmatics should do the special program in Part III before undertaking the Foundation Lessons.

Note: As you practice conscious breathing activities, you may notice that your heartbeat speeds up on your in-breath and slows down on your out-breath. This pattern is entirely normal, although it goes by the unwieldy medical name of respiratory sinus arrhythmia.

FOUNDATION LESSON ONE

Exploring Your Breathing from the Inside Out

In this lesson you will discover how your breathing works from inside and outside your body. You will bring consciousness to the physiological mechanisms of your breathing, using your own awareness as your exploratory tool. Many people have found that this internal anatomy lesson has considerable healing power all its own. Simply by learning how your breathing works and is designed to work, you will have a firm base from which to mount deeper explorations to come.

INSTRUCTIONS

To begin, find a firm but giving surface upon which you can lie down. A carpeted floor is perfect for this and the other lying-down activities in this book. If lying down is not convenient or feasible for you, you may sit up in a chair. Light clothing is ideal. Remove heavy sweaters, constricting belts, and any other clothing that might interfere with this activity.

Lie down with your arms resting at your sides. Let your feet be a comfortable distance apart. If you like, you can rest your neck and head on a small pillow. You also may feel more comfortable with a pillow under your knees. You can close your eyes or leave them open, whichever is more comfortable for you.

We are going to do something in this lesson that you may never have done before. We are going to take an internal guided tour of some key parts of your breathing anatomy, using your own consciousness as the searchlight. Conscious breathing starts with a conscious feeling-picture of how your breathing works and why it is designed the way it is.

Let's begin by noticing the beautifully efficient structure of your rib cage. Bring your hands up so that you can feel your collarbones with your fingertips.

Run your fingers along your collarbones from the outside, where they touch into your shoulders, to where they join into your sternum or breastbone. Tap your collarbone rapidly and gently. Tap it from

FIGURE 2.

The Beginning Position for Foundation Lesson One

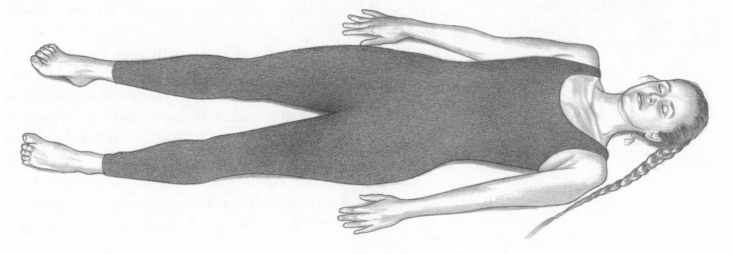

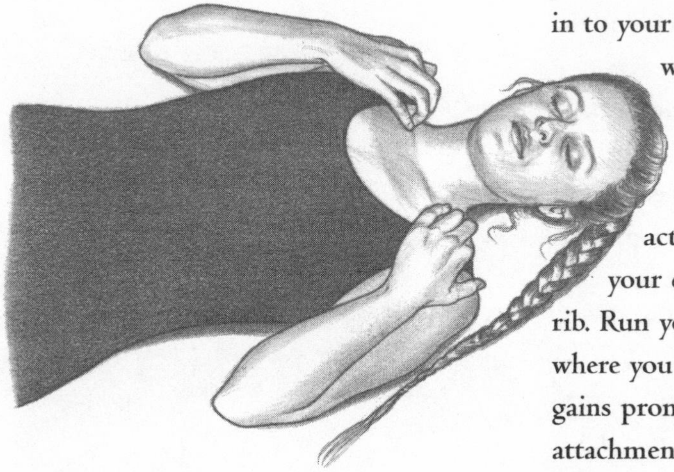

FIGURE 3.

Touching Your Collarbones

where it joins the shoulders to where it connects to the sternum. After you have tapped it for fifteen or twenty seconds, pause and simply tune in to your collarbone. With your attention, feel your collarbone all the way from shoulder to sternum.

Explore again with your fingers. See if you can feel the points where your collarbone connects to your sternum. The rib you can feel clearly just beneath your collarbone is actually your second rib. Your first rib is hidden underneath your collarbone and cannot be felt in its entirety. Feel your second rib. Run your fingertips along it now. Start out toward your shoulders, where you can't actually feel it, and run your fingers along until the rib gains prominence and joins your sternum. Feel how solid and sure that attachment feels. With your fingers resting on the place where your second rib joins the sternum, take a big breath and feel your ribs move. Your rib cage is a solid structure, but it also has exquisite flexibility. Take another deep breath and feel the movement of your ribs with your fingertips.

Slowly trace down your sternum with your fingertips. Feel where each rib joins the sternum. Notice that the farther down the sternum you go, the closer the ribs are together. Keep following the sternum down until it ends. Feel just beneath the sternum, at the very bottom of it. There is a tiny bone here called the xiphoid process. Many people have a sensitivity here; it feels "funny" to the touch. It has every right to feel sensitive. It is connected to the diaphragm, one of the most sensitive and important structures in your body. We'll do a more detailed exploration of the diaphragm in just a moment.

Now trace your rib cage with your fingers as it continues on down. Feel how far it goes. Gently and rapidly tap the edge of your rib cage with your fingertips, all the way from your xiphoid process down to where you can feel the bottom of your ribs. Pause and feel the boundaries of your rib cage from inside, with your attention. Notice that the bottom of your ribs is all the way down by your waist. Many of us think of our lungs as high up in our chest, but in fact your lungs follow the structure of the rib cage you have just traced. Your lungs are relatively small at the top and very large at the bottom. That is why in our lessons we will focus a great deal on learning to breathe deeply into the belly, so that we take advantage of how nature has designed us. Most of the blood circulating in the lungs is in the bottom third of them. Yet many of us, when we go to take a deep breath, breathe high up into the chest rather than deeply into our bellies. Breathing high up in the chest actually defeats the purpose of the big breath. We will definitely correct that tendency in our lessons.

Now rest your hands at your sides, and use your consciousness to do what your hands have just done. Sense how your collarbone connects to your sternum. With your attention, feel your sternum and follow it down until you can feel the xiphoid process at the very bottom of it. Now sense the bottom of your rib cage all the way down on both sides. Notice how far down your ribs go, all the way down near your waist on both sides. Take several deep breaths, feeling how your rib cage moves with each breath.

Now we will find out more about that diaphragm muscle that we

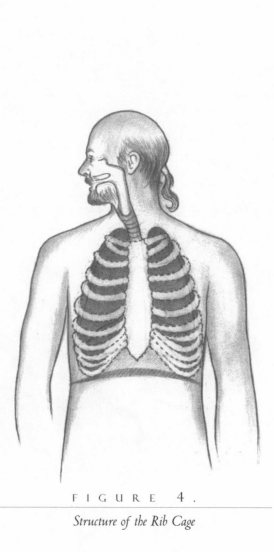

FIGURE 4.

Structure of the Rib Cage

said was so important. Place your fingertips together along the shape of your lower rib cage.

Your diaphragm is shaped like a dome. When you breathe in, the dome flattens. Let your fingers flatten your imaginary dome as you breathe in.

When you breathe out, the diaphragm resumes its rounded dome shape again. Breathe out, and round your imaginary dome with your fingers.

Let your hands mimic the movement of the diaphragm through several breathing cycles. Take a slow, deep in-breath while flattening the dome shape you have made with your fingers. Then let the breath out, and let your fingers round upward into a dome shape again. This will give you a sense of how the diaphragm operates. When you breathe in, your diaphragm actually contracts and goes downward. Then your diaphragm relaxes and resumes its rounded shape on your out-breath.

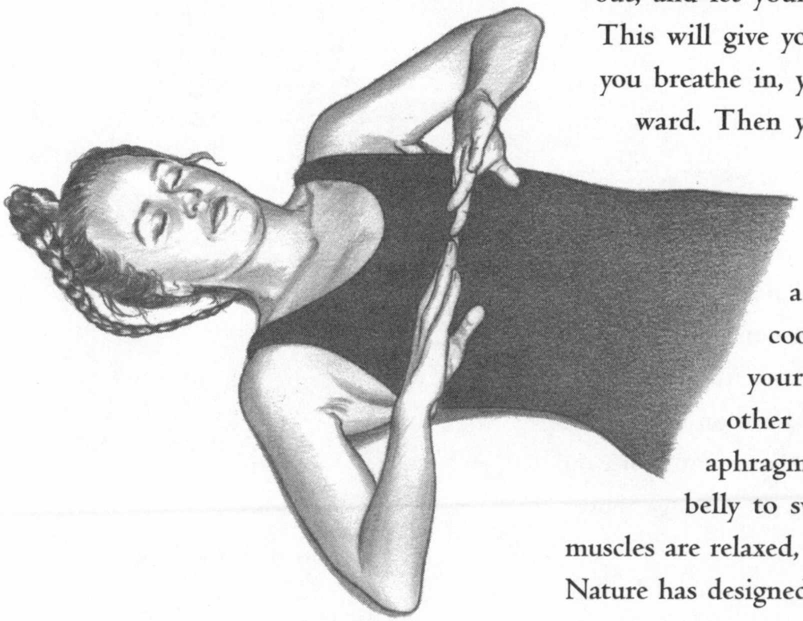

And here is where something crucial must happen. For effective breathing to take place, your diaphragm and your abdominal muscles must cooperate. Let's find out how. Put your hands now on your abdomen, one hand just above your navel, the other hand just below. When you breathe in, your diaphragm flattens and pushes downward. This causes your belly to swell out with the in-breath. Ideally, your stomach muscles are relaxed, so that when you breathe in, your stomach rounds. Nature has designed it this way. You breathe in and your belly rounds,

FIGURE 5A.

The Shape of Your Diaphragm During Inhalation

creating a massage for the vital organs in the abdomen. But what if your stomach muscles are so tight that you cannot fully allow a deep breath to occur? Unfortunately, this is a problem that plagues many people. The diaphragm cannot flatten all the way as it is supposed to. You cannot take a full breath. Many physical problems, such as high blood pressure, are partly the result of having tight stomach muscles and not being able to take a full breath.

Let's exaggerate the movement of the diaphragm and stomach muscles for a moment to get a sense of their full range of motion. Take a big breath into your chest and hold it. Don't let any breath out for a moment. Imagine the pressure in your chest as a ball of breath. Push this ball down so that your stomach bulges out. Then push it back up into your chest by contracting your stomach muscles. Rock or bounce this ball of pressure back and forth from chest to belly several times. See if you can do it while keeping the rest of your body relaxed. After you've done this a few times, let the breath go and breathe normally. Pause and rest for a moment. Take a few big, easy breaths into your relaxed center.

Now let's get a sense of why your diaphragm usually doesn't get to move through its full range of motion. Find out what your stomach muscles feel like when they are tense. To do this, we will consciously re-create part of the fight-or-flight reflex. Feel your abdomen with your hands. As you rest your hands on your abdomen, lift your head up a few inches off the floor. Feel the muscles of your abdomen tighten.

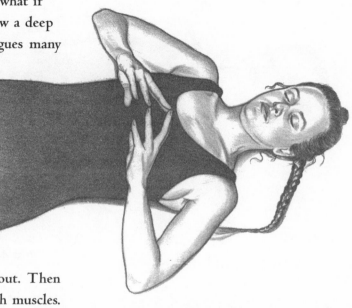

FIGURE 5 B.

The Shape of Your Diaphragm During Exhalation

FIGURE 6.

Marking the Extent of the Abdominal Muscles: From Deep in the Pelvis to the Chest

In the fight-or-flight reflex, your head comes forward and your belly tightens. In this position, with your head lifted off the floor, try to take a deep breath. Feel how difficult it is. Now relax your head back on the floor. Take several deep breaths into your abdomen, keeping your stomach muscles very soft. This is the opposite of the fight-or-flight reflex.

Let's explore this more deeply. With your fingertips, touch the area just below your xiphoid process with one hand and just above your pubic bone with your other hand.

Now lift your head again a few inches off the floor. Notice that your abdominal muscles go all the way from your pubic bone up into your chest. These are the muscles that need to stay very relaxed so that you can take a full breath. And these are the very muscles that get tight when we are scared. Nature has designed it so that any animal freezes its breathing and tightens its muscles when it perceives threat. In the wild, this move has a great deal of survival value. It mobilizes the animal to run or fight back—the famous fight-or-flight reflex—and it makes the animal very still so that it is less likely to be seen.

Tightening the abdominal muscles also protects the soft organs inside. If you are about to receive a blow, it is to your advantage to tighten your muscle wall so that the vital organs inside will not be hurt. But most of us don't live in the wild anymore. Most of us are not in situations where receiving a physical blow is likely. Nor is it feasible

for us to run or fight physically. Nowadays most of the threats we receive are social in nature—we fear criticism or embarrassment or making a mistake. But we've still got this same physiology that came into
being hundreds of thousands of years ago. In other words, we are dealing with the problems of civilization with a nervous system that was
designed in the jungle. It can work just fine if we learn to use it more
creatively. We can start by noticing situations where we tighten our abdominal muscles and restrict our breathing.

Back to the body now. Let's consciously and slowly re-create more of
the fight-or-flight reflex. Rest your arms at your sides. Now lift your
head off the floor a few inches or so, and feel your stomach muscles
tighten. As you lift your head, make fists and hunch your shoulders.
Hold this position for a moment and study it carefully. We are exagger-
ating it, but this is exactly what happens if you feel threatened,
whether it's by hearing a startling noise or getting chewed out by your
boss. Try to take a few deep breaths while holding this position. Take a
very clear mental and kinesthetic snapshot of what it feels like to have
your breathing restricted by tight stomach muscles. Now relax your
head back on the floor, and rest your arms again at your sides. Take a
moment to rest and relax any tension in your body.

Now let's consciously create the fight-or-flight reflex in its entirety.
Do these four things all at once: Lift your head off the floor, make
tight fists, hunch your shoulders, and tense your buttocks. Hold this
position for a moment so that you can take a kinesthetic snapshot of
it. Try to take a few deep breaths in the midst of all this tension. Now
rest again on the floor. Rest your arms at your sides, and let all your

muscles relax. Take a few deep breaths into your relaxed abdomen, feeling it swell as you breathe in and flatten as you breathe out.

Before we finish our first Foundation Lesson, let's explore one more aspect of your breathing physiology. Place your hands on your abdomen again. Rest one hand between your navel and pubic bone, the other hand between your navel and xiphoid process. Let your hands ride up and down on your relaxed abdomen for a few breathing cycles.

Now, take a big breath in, and hold it for a moment. Purse your lips and imagine you are blowing out all the candles on a birthday cake as you blow out your breath. Did you feel your stomach muscles tighten as you blew out the breath? Do it again twice more. Take a big in-breath, then blow out the breath as if you were blowing out birthday candles. Feel how a strong out-breath contracts your stomach muscles, then relax your stomach muscles completely as you breathe in. Now rest for a moment and contemplate this awareness.

Nature has designed you so that you have powerful muscles to blow breath out but not to breathe it in. Few of us would try to extinguish our birthday candles by sucking in air. Some theorists think that powerful exhaling muscles developed so that we could dislodge food stuck in the windpipe. Regardless of where this ability came from, it is clear that we have a much stronger ability to breathe out than to breathe in. What we need to learn from this is simple but quite significant: Keep your in-breath very relaxed. It is perfectly fine to use a little tightening of the stomach muscles at the end of the out-breath, but make sure you relax your stomach muscles completely on the in-breath.

Let's explore this right now. Keep your hands on your abdomen so that you can feel your stomach muscles. At the end of the out-breath, tighten your stomach muscles a little, as if you were going to squeeze all the breath out. Then relax your stomach muscles completely as you breathe in. Repeat this sequence a few times: Breathe all the way out, tightening the stomach muscles slightly at the end as if to squeeze the last drop of air out. Then relax completely as you fill the belly with air. Keep it easy and gentle. You do not need to use much effort at all—just a subtle little squeeze at the end of the out-breath. Then relax completely as you breathe into your rounded abdomen.

Continue with this pattern for a minute or two, then rest until you feel like resuming your normal activities.

This concludes Foundation Lesson One.

Cultivating Full Diaphragmatic Breathing

This lesson will show you how to get your breath farther down into your abdomen, moving your diaphragm through its full range of motion. It contains some of the most important information I have learned in two decades as a healer. If I am limited to only one contact with a given client, I usually teach the person this lesson. I have found very few people who do not need to learn this material. Interestingly, I have worked with many people—such as opera singers, professional athletes, and ballet dancers—who use their breath to make their living. Sometimes these people make the greatest improvement in the shortest period of time through this Foundation Lesson. So whether you are a beginner or an "old pro" breather, I recommend that you study and practice this lesson often, as I do.

I first caught on to the power of full diaphragmatic breathing through watching babies breathe. There was a time, early in my study of breathing, when I assigned myself the task of watching a hundred babies breathe. This study was crucial to my understanding, because it showed me what healthy breathing was supposed to look like. My daughter was in elementary school at the time, so I extended my observations to children up through the sixth grade. I was amazed to see that healthy breathing gradually disappeared as children grew older. I rarely saw a baby who could not breathe diaphragmatically, but I rarely saw a sixth-grader who could. Something happens along the way, in the socialization process, that causes many of us to develop fight-or-flight breathing, or what I call upside-down breathing.

Upside-down breathing is, as the name implies, the reverse of healthy breathing. In healthy diaphragmatic breathing, the belly muscles are relaxed, allowing the abdomen to swell with the in-breath. There is relatively little movement in the chest in relaxed breathing, nor does there need to be. Recall that less than a teacup of blood circulates in the upper portion of the lungs every minute. The chest needs to move a lot only when you are exerting yourself.

When you are scared, the fight-or-flight reflex tightens your belly muscles, so that there is no room for your diaphragm to go through its full range of motion. This forces your breath up into your chest. Healthy breathing equals relaxed abdominal muscles and room for the diaphragm to move. Unhealthy breathing equals tight belly and compensatory inflation of the chest. Hence, it is upside-down. When I ask new clients to take a deep breath, nine times out of ten they will take a big, exaggerated breath up into their chests, sucking in their bellies by tightening their abdominal muscles. This is upside-down breathing at work.

There are actually several reasons why upside-down breathing occurs. We have mentioned that much of it stems from fear and the fight-or-flight reflex. But there are other reasons. One is in the cultural taboo against rounded bellies. Fashion dictates that both men and women must have flat bellies. The gaunt fashion-model look still has power over certain segments of the population, as does the ramrod-straight military-inspired look for men. It was not uncommon in the nineteenth century for young women to die from corset-inflicted mutilation of their vital organs.

There are passionate denunciations of corsets in medical journals of that era. We still have not recovered from this problem, although corsets have mercifully gone out of fashion.

Not long ago I was getting a haircut in a new and trendy salon, when I noticed that my haircutter had not smiled or taken a diaphragmatic breath since I had been there. I made mention of this, and she readily agreed, although she was surprised that I had noticed it. She said she made a point of taking very shallow breaths, even though the practice made her "feel tired all the time." I asked her why and was astounded by her answer. She said that taking deep breaths made her "look fat." This was coming from a twenty-year-old who was nearly anorexically thin. But why the deadpan, poker-faced expression? Surely, smiling didn't make her look fat, did it? No, but her answer was equally horrifying: Smiling made her face wrinkle. I hope this is an extreme and rare case, but I am afraid that it is not. All too many of us in this culture pay so much attention to how we look from outside that we stunt the growth of our inner experience.

There is no question that tight clothing—especially tight belts—restrict the movement of the abdomen and diaphragm. At our institute, I would estimate that nearly half the people who practice our breathing programs must be asked to remove or loosen a belt or other piece of clothing that is hindering their full breathing. In light of this, I would recommend that you review the contents of your closet, to make sure your clothes are not only pleasing but also "breather-friendly."

Another case that I have seen many times is diaphragmatic breathing that has been frozen by trauma to the abdomen. If you have been injured in your abdomen, and especially if you have had any surgery in that general area, you may have learned to breathe around the trauma rather than through it. I have worked with several hundred people who were recovering from abdominal surgery—hysterectomies, hernia repair, appendectomies, cesarean sections—and I have yet to see one whose breathing was not hindered by the surgery. Generally speaking, it takes two to three weeks of conscious breathing work to get your breathing back on track after something as traumatic as surgery. Not only do you have the physical wound of the trauma to recover from, but anesthesia is also a major factor.

When I hurt my leg in the mid-eighties, I had a three-hour operation under general anesthesia. I did an hour of conscious breathing every day for several weeks after the surgery, and I was still smelling anesthesia coming off my breath for two of those weeks. Anesthesia has a strong effect on the breathing mechanisms of the body, particularly the diaphragm. Strange as it seems, I have smelled anesthesialike gases coming off the breath of people who have not had surgery in years. I was mystified when this first happened. How could a gas stay trapped in the body so long? One day I hope to capture some of it in a balloon and take it to a lab for analysis. It would interest me to find out whether it is actually anesthetic or some natural chemical, such as a ketone, that just happens to be emitted.

To conclude, there are many reasons why we lose the skill and talent of full diaphragmatic breathing. But there are only a few things you need to know and practice to get it back again. The purpose of Foundation Lesson Two is to recover healthy diaphragmatic breathing, so that every breath you take will be a source of health and even pleasure.

INSTRUCTIONS

Our lesson comes in two parts: a lying-down phase and a sitting-up phase. The reason for this is simple. Healthy diaphragmatic breathing

is easiest to learn lying down, but most of us will need it most sitting or standing upright in gravity. So we will first hone the skill lying down, then learn how to practice it in normal life situations.

Breathing feels a little different lying down from the way it does sitting or standing. This is because when you are lying down, you have to lift the heft of the abdomen with each in-breath. The weight of the abdomen, though, makes the out-breath easier. These are not factors when you are sitting or standing.

F I G U R E   7 .

When Breathing on Your Back, Your In-Breath Lifts the Weight of Your Abdomen

Part One

Let's begin by lying down on your back with your hands at your sides. Let your feet be a comfortable distance apart. Take a moment to get comfortable there. You can close your eyes or keep them open, whichever is more comfortable for you.

There are two things a healthy baby does when it breathes. First, its stomach muscles are relaxed so that it can take a full-belly-

breath, and second, its spine flexes in a certain way with each breath. A full diaphragmatic breath not only rounds the belly but moves the spine in a specific way. This lesson will show you how to put this "healthy baby" breathing to work for you.

Bring your legs up so that your knees are bent and your feet are flat on the floor. Make sure your feet are a comfortable width apart and a comfortable distance from your buttocks. Do your best to find a position that allows your legs to feel balanced and relaxed. If at any time your legs get tired of being in this position, stretch them out for a moment to rest them.

Begin to arch the small of your back gently, then flatten it again on the floor. Keep doing this very slowly, taking several seconds to arch the small of your back, then several more seconds to flatten the small of the back against the floor. Make it a smooth, gentle, meditative movement, not short or choppy. Sense and feel the tiny sensations of the movement as you arch and flatten the small of your back.

Now begin to take a deep, slow round-belly-breath as you arch the small of your back, and a deep, slow out-breath as you flatten the small of your back. Breathe in and fill your belly as you arch the small of your back, then breathe

FIGURE 8 .

On the In-Breath, Gently Arch the Small of Your Back as You Fill Your Belly

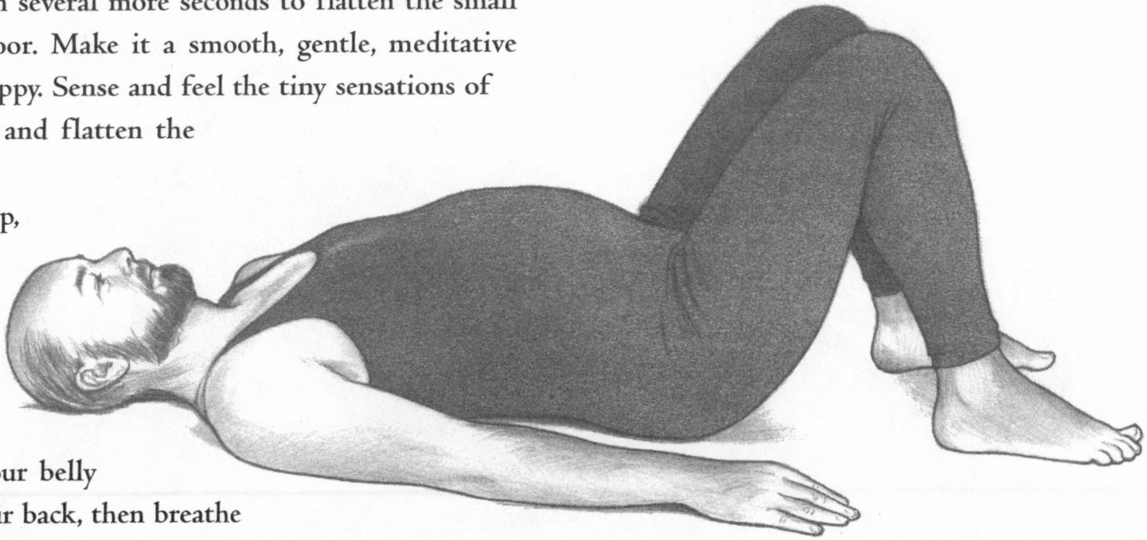

out fully as you flatten the small of your back. Keep it slow and gentle. It doesn't need to be a huge movement—just a few inches of arching and flattening.

As you continue this, let your attention go to your tailbone. Sense the movement of your tailbone as you breathe. As you arch the small of your back and breathe into your rounded belly, notice that your tailbone is rolling down the floor toward its tip, the coccyx. As you breathe out and flatten your back, notice that your tailbone is rolling up the floor toward where it joins your spine. Breathe slowly for a few cycles, keeping your awareness focused on your tailbone. Sense how this often-forgotten part of your body is linked perfectly to each breath you take.

Continue this movement very slowly and consciously—take a full round-belly-breath as you arch the small of your back, and a complete out-breath as you flatten the small of your back. As you do, place your hands at the bottom of your rib cage, right where it joins your waist at the sides.

As your breathing continues, notice with your hands that your abdomen swells to the front and to the sides on the in-breath. As the dome of your dia-

FIGURE 9.

On the Out-Breath, Flatten the Small of Your Back

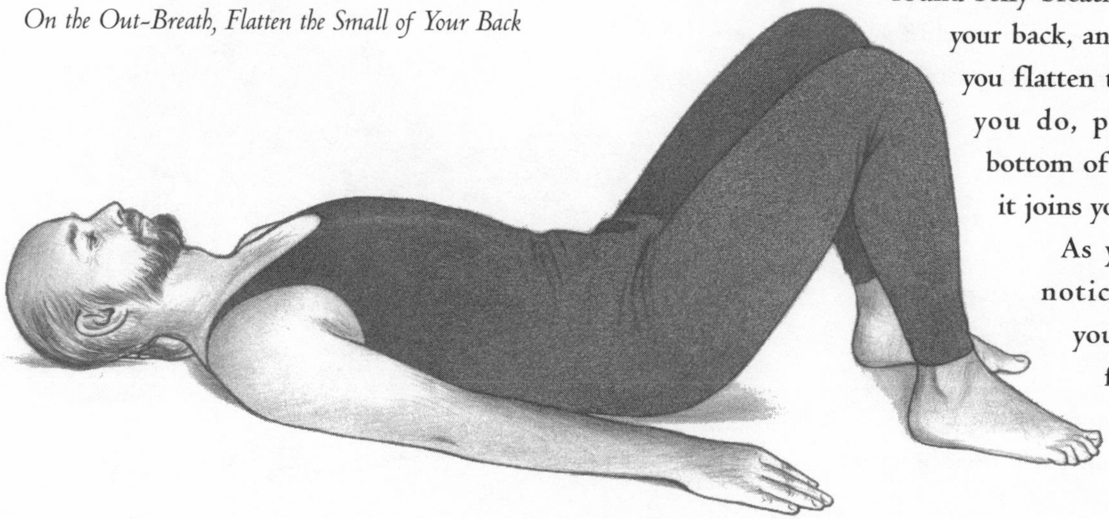

phragm flattens on your in-breath, your abdomen swells in several directions—to the front, to the side, even to the back. Feel the filling of your abdomen with each in-breath, and its narrowing as you breathe out. Visualize what is happening inside your body as you breathe. When you breathe in, arching the small of your back slightly, your diaphragm flattens down toward your abdominal cavity. If your stomach muscles are relaxed, your belly will swell, giving your vital organs room to breathe. As you breathe out, your diaphragm rounds into its dome shape up toward your chest cavity. All the while, your spine is flexing with each breath. This is exactly the way nature has designed it, so that you will get a spinal stretch and an organ massage with each breath. By breathing this way, you bathe the inside of your body with freshly oxygenated blood while keeping your spine limber and free.

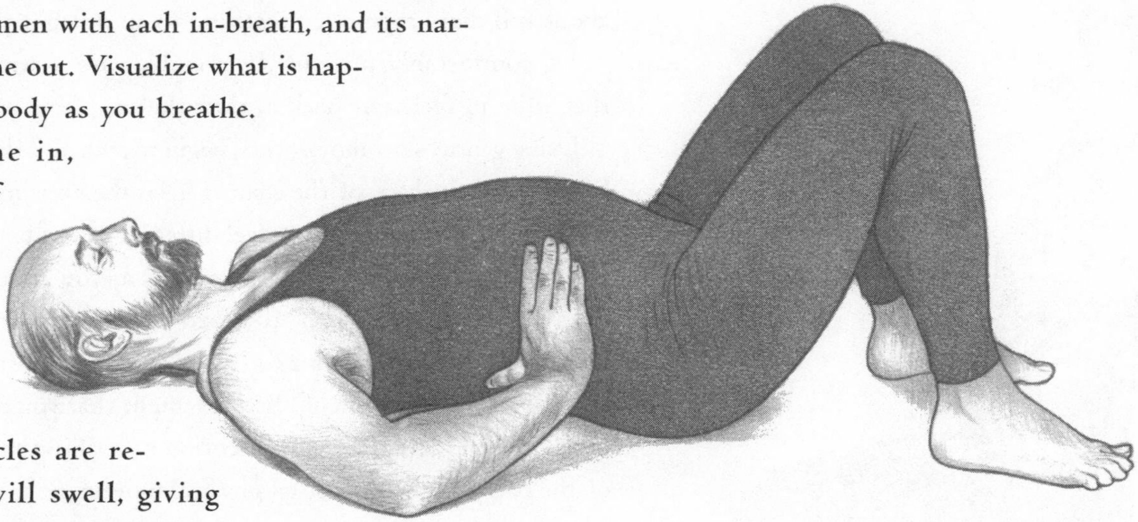

Practice for another minute or two, then relax and rest.

Notice how your body feels now, compared to when you first lay down.

FIGURE 10.

Feel How Your Abdomen Swells to the Front, Sides, and Back with Each In-Breath

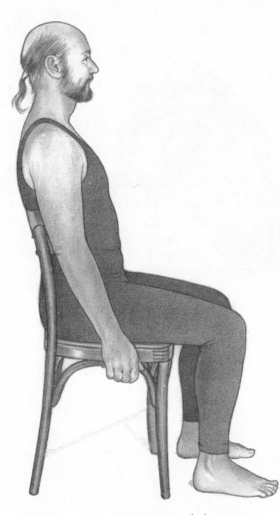

FIGURE 11.

*Bringing Full Diaphragmatic Breathing to a
Seated Position*

Part Two

Now let us explore how you can translate what you have learned about full diaphragmatic breathing to an upright position.

Sit comfortably upright. If possible, use a straight-backed chair so that you can feel your back against the support.

Using gentle, slow movements, begin to arch and flatten the small of your back against the back of the chair. This is the same movement you were just doing on the floor, but it may feel different to you because of your different relationship to gravity. Notice now that as you arch and flatten the small of your back, you roll forward and back on your "sit-bones." Do this movement first in a full, even exaggerated way several times. Then shift to a subtle version of the movement that you could do without anyone noticing. Have the inner intention of arching and flattening the small of the back, but do the actual physical movement so quietly that you could do it in a group without attracting attention.

Now let's add the breath to the movement. Go back to doing the movement in a full but still gentle way. As you arch the small of your back, breathe in and let your belly round. As you flatten the small of your back, breathe out and flatten your belly. Feel how relaxed you can get your belly on the in-breath. Let the abdomen fall out and down as you breathe in. Don't worry about what it looks like from outside. Focus on the inner experience of your stomach muscles staying very relaxed as you breathe.

Place your hands at the bottom of your rib cage, as you did before when you were lying down.

Feel with your hands that your abdomen expands to the front and to the sides as you breathe in. As you breathe out, feel your abdomen become narrower. Do several cycles of slow, easy, full breaths, feeling your abdomen swell and narrow with your breath. When you breathe in, breathe down and into your rounded abdomen. When you breathe out, do a complete exhalation, one that clears all the breath out of your body.

After a few more cycles, pause and rest for a moment or two before resuming your normal activities.

This concludes Foundation Lesson Two.

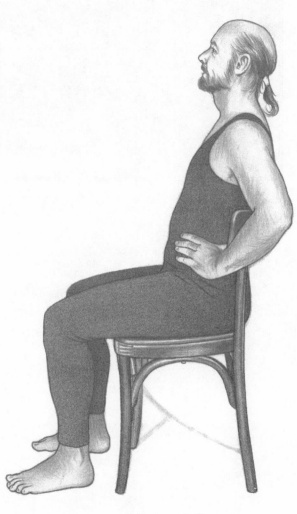

FIGURE 12.

Feel How the Abdomen Moves with Full Diaphragmatic Breathing

Breathing for Mind/Body Integration

I like to give people a breathing practice right away in which they can feel a shift in their state of consciousness. Often, in my first session with a new client, I teach this practice—what one of my clients called her "five-minute miracle"—because it produces such beneficial and rapid results.

The difference between the two sides of the cerebral cortex is one of the most fascinating scientific discoveries of the past twenty-five years. If you place your hands on the top of your head so that your fingertips touch, you will be covering the area of the two hemispheres of your cortex. The two hemispheres are connected by a thick bundle of fibers, the corpus callosum, which resembles a telephone cable. Many of the language functions of the brain are on the left side, while the picture-making functions are located in the right hemisphere. The phrase *right-hemisphere* has come to symbolize feeling, emotion, imagery, and intuition, while *left-hemisphere* has come to refer to logic, mathematics, words, and linear thinking.

The left side of the nose is connected to the right side of the brain, and vice versa. Breathing alternately through each nostril causes a shift from one hemisphere of the brain to the other. In this lesson we will draw on this phenomenon of physiology. My sense is that shifting hemispheres is what gives the practice its power. Switching from one brain hemisphere to another a number of times, while breathing slowly and deeply, seems to bring about a balance. My personal experience has shown me that it improves mood, refreshes the body, and sharpens the mind.

One of the first conscious breathing experiments I ever did made use of alternate-nostril breathing, which is a traditional yoga practice. Since that first time I have tried out dozens of different variations, arriving finally at the one I will show you in this lesson. I have practiced and taught it many thousands of times now, with uniformly excellent results. In fact, I know of nothing that will shift a tired or scattered mood more quickly than this practice. Done properly, it reliably produces a clear, calm, and focused state of mind. It is a more subtle activity than either of the ones you have done thus far; take care to do it mindfully and slowly, getting the instructions just right.

This lesson contains two parts: an initial experiment, followed by an advanced version of the practice. You can do them both in the same session, or save the second part for another time.

INSTRUCTIONS

This lesson is best done sitting upright. Take a moment to get comfortably seated. You may do this lesson with your eyes open or closed, whichever is more comfortable for you.

Let's begin with your dominant hand. In other words, if you are right-handed, use your right hand. Later, we will switch to your nondominant hand. Place your thumb of that hand on one side of your nose and your middle finger on the other side. I usually rest my index finger on my forehead, making a tripod. Find a position that is comfortable for you.

Alternately close one nostril then the other a few times, to get the feel of it. Do it gently and slowly, mindful of the sensitivity of your nose.

The practice goes like this: Begin on the out-breath. Breathe out and back in on one side, then close that nostril and switch to the other side, breathing out and back in. You always switch nostrils before the out-breath. Try it a few times. Breathe slowly and gently out, then easily back in on that side Now close that nostril and breathe out and in on the other side. Switch, breathing out and in on the other side. Always do it with the out-breath first. I've tried it many different ways, and this is the one that produces the best results.

As you practice, focus on the sensations of the breath as it goes out

FIGURE 13.

The Hand Position for Alternate-Nostril Breathing

of your nose and comes back in. Keep your stomach muscles relaxed. Breathe slowly and deeply in and out of your relaxed abdomen. Take care not to use much effort. Just breathe easily and naturally as you switch nostrils before each out-breath.

Practice now uninterruptedly for two minutes. Keep the breath slow and gentle, and focus your mind on the sensations of the air coming in and out of your nose.

After your two minutes are up, switch to your nondominant hand. Use your nondominant hand to alternately close each nostril. Practice for two more minutes with this hand.

After your two minutes of practice with your nondominant hand, switch back to your dominant hand to finish. Practice one minute with your dominant hand.

When you feel finished, rest your hands at your sides or in your lap. Rest for a minute or so before resuming your normal activities.

An Advanced Alternate-Nostril Practice

Now we will add a new element to your alternate-nostril breathing: lengthening the breath. If you are using conscious breathing to get more relaxed, it is to your advantage to breathe very slowly. It is difficult to feel relaxed if you are breathing that fast. In order to feel a deep sense of calm in your body, you will want to slow your breathing down to between six and ten breaths per minute. This activity is a simple way to get your breathing slowed down.

INSTRUCTIONS

Sit comfortably upright. Place your dominant hand as you did before, with your thumb on one side of your nose and your middle finger on the other side. Just as you did before, begin breathing out and back in on one side, then switch to the other nostril to breathe out and back in. Do this for a few cycles.

Now let's begin to lengthen and slow your breathing. On the out-breath, mentally count to four slowly. Make each count last about a second: Out-2-3-4, In-2-3-4. Then switch nostrils and repeat: Out-2-3-4, In-2-3-4. An old trick for counting seconds is to say, "One thousand ONE, one thousand TWO, one thousand THREE, one thousand FOUR." Use this four-count breathing now for the next two minutes.

When your two minutes are up, switch to your nondominant hand. After you get your hand established, begin to use a five-count. Out-2-3-4-5, In-2-3-4-5. Practice with your nondominant hand for two minutes.

If you lose count or need a breath sooner, just go back and start with the counting when you are ready.

After two minutes with your nondominant hand, switch back to your dominant hand for one minute of practice.

On subsequent occasions you may want to extend this practice to a six-count, seven-count, eight-count, or longer. I routinely use an eight-count now, meaning that I am only breathing three or four times a minute.

When you feel finished, rest for a minute or two before resuming your normal activities.

This concludes Foundation Lesson Three.

CHAPTER 4

Five Advanced Lessons in Conscious Breathing

IN MANY ANCIENT CULTURES BREATH WAS SYNONYMOUS WITH SPIRIT. To the Greeks, spirit was *pneuma*, the feeling of the breath moving in the body. To the Romans it was *spiritus* and to the Hindus *atman*, the very feeling of God in the body. The enlivening feeling of the moving breath occupies a special place in the human experience. Breath is more to us than air: It is life itself, the feeling that lets us know that we are here. In the second chapter of Genesis, God created the first human and "breathed into his nostrils the breath of life; and man became a living soul."

Breathing also occupies a special place because it is on the borderline between the known and the unknown. You can will yourself consciously to take a deep breath, then you can go to the opposite extreme and let your unconscious do it for you. You can even go to sleep for eight hours,

Prana is the breath of life of all beings in the universe. They are born through it and live by it, and when they die their individual breath dissolves into the cosmic breath.

—B.K.S. JYENGAR

and your breathing will go about its business on its own. Breathing occupies the border between the conscious and the unconscious. This is a borderland that human beings have loved to explore for thousands of years. One of the oldest books I've held in my hands is a four-thousand-year-old document from the Kashmiri yoga tradition. It contains instructions on how to take a full breath so that the spirit is nurtured.

In this chapter we will go deeply into the borderland between body and spirit, using breath as our means of locomotion and consciousness as our guide. As in the Foundation Lessons in Chapter 3, use your comfort as your counselor. All these activities are designed to be done in the comfort zone. Don't push, don't try too hard, certainly don't strain or create tension in your body. If you find that you are producing any discomfort through your conscious breathing—tension, dizziness, pain—let that be your signal to pause and lighten up until you can bring ease back into your breathing.

Now, set aside a little quiet time each day and begin to explore the treasures of these advanced practices.

Opening Space in Your Body for Deeper Breathing

As you go more deeply into your breathing, you will find that your old habits have created limits in your body that must be transcended. These limits become ingrained in the body but they can be unlearned with some conscious practice. In this lesson we will use subtle movements to open up more territory for your breathing to occupy.

Many of these lessons are informed and inspired by Wilhelm Reich and Moshe Feldenkrais, two geniuses of our century. It was through Feldenkrais in particular that I learned the power of using creative, conscious movements—done very slowly—to open the breath. The value of this lesson depends on your willingness to practice it gently and thoughtfully, more like a meditation than an exercise.

INSTRUCTIONS

This lesson is done lying down. Find yourself a comfortable, firm surface to rest on, and lie down on your back. You will need room enough to stretch out your arms to the side in a little while.

Bring up your legs, knees bent, feet flat on the floor.

Let's begin by doing a minute or so of the basic diaphragmatic breathing you learned in Foundation Lesson Two. As you breathe in slowly and deeply, round your belly as you arch the small of your back. As you breathe out, flatten your back against the floor. Focus on the sensations of the breath in your body, going for smooth, easy movements.

(Pause now and practice for a minute.)

Now, let's practice a simple, gentle movement that will open up more space in the front of your body. Many of the restrictions in your breath come from muscular holding patterns. Our old tensions and pains cause us to move our muscles less. Since our breathing requires open space and flexible muscles, we gradually breathe less deeply in response to these tight muscles. Attempts to stretch muscles forcefully often do more harm than good. Instead, we will use very gentle, conscious movements to relax the muscles and create more breathing space.

Place your arms straight out to the sides in a T-formation. Rest your hands on their palms.

Breathe as you did before, using basic diaphragmatic breathing. But now we will add an arm movement that opens up the chest at the same time. Breathe in and arch the small of your back, and at the same time

FIGURE 14.

Beginning Position

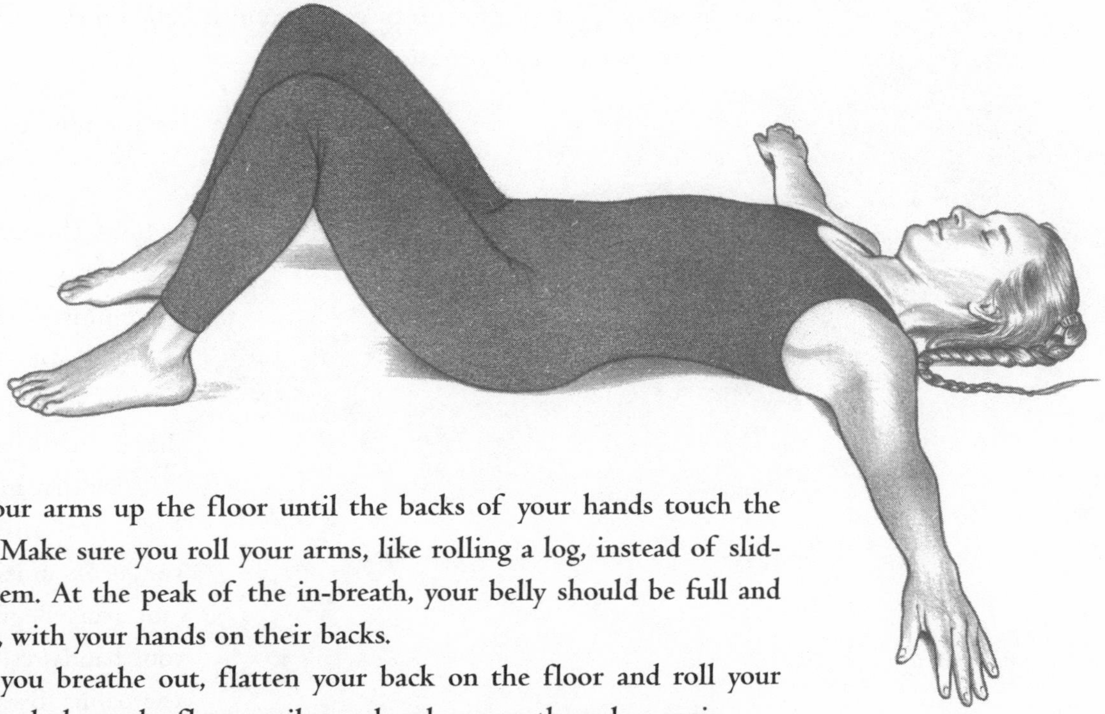

FIGURE 15.

Begin with Your Palms Down

roll your arms up the floor until the backs of your hands touch the floor. Make sure you roll your arms, like rolling a log, instead of sliding them. At the peak of the in-breath, your belly should be full and round, with your hands on their backs.

As you breathe out, flatten your back on the floor and roll your arms back down the floor until your hands are on the palms again.

Now take ten to fifteen slow breaths, repeating the sequence. You breathe into your rounded stomach at the same time as you roll both arms up the floor, until your hands rest on their backs. Then you breathe out as you roll your arms back down the floor, until your palms are back where they started. For now, make it a small movement, just a few inches of movement with your arms. Feel the sensations of your chest opening and expanding, gently stretching and relaxing the pectoral muscles at the edge of your chest up near your shoulders. As your breath goes deep down into your rounded belly on the in-breath, your chest opens simultaneously.

(Pause and practice for ten to fifteen breaths.)

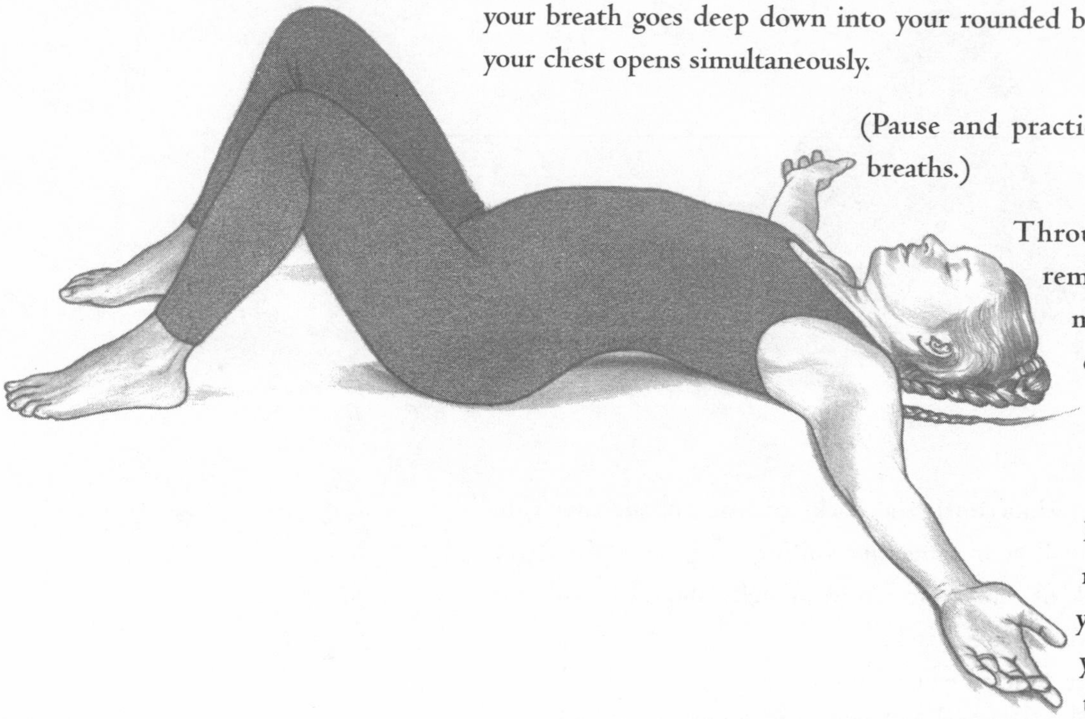

Throughout this activity, remember to keep your movements in the comfort zone. Don't strain or try too hard.

With that in mind, let's expand the range of motion of your arms. Begin with your hands resting on the palms. Breathe as you did before, arching the small of the back as you round your belly on the in-breath, then flattening the small of the back against the floor as you breathe out. This time, though, find out how far up the floor your arms will roll on the in-breath, and how far down the floor they'll roll on the out-breath. As you breathe in, roll your arms up the floor and go past the point where your hands were on their backs. Go as far as you comfortably can, then roll your arms back down the floor on your out-breath. Keep repeating this movement as you breathe, always staying in your comfort zone. If you stay in this comfort zone,

FIGURE 16.

On the In-Breath, Roll Your Arms Up the Floor, Opening Your Chest as You Fill Your Belly

you will probably find that the spiral movement of your arms is a little bigger every few breaths. Keep finding the upper limit of how gently and easily you can roll your arms up with the in-breath, then back down the floor on the out-breath.

(Pause and practice this sequence for ten to fifteen breaths.)

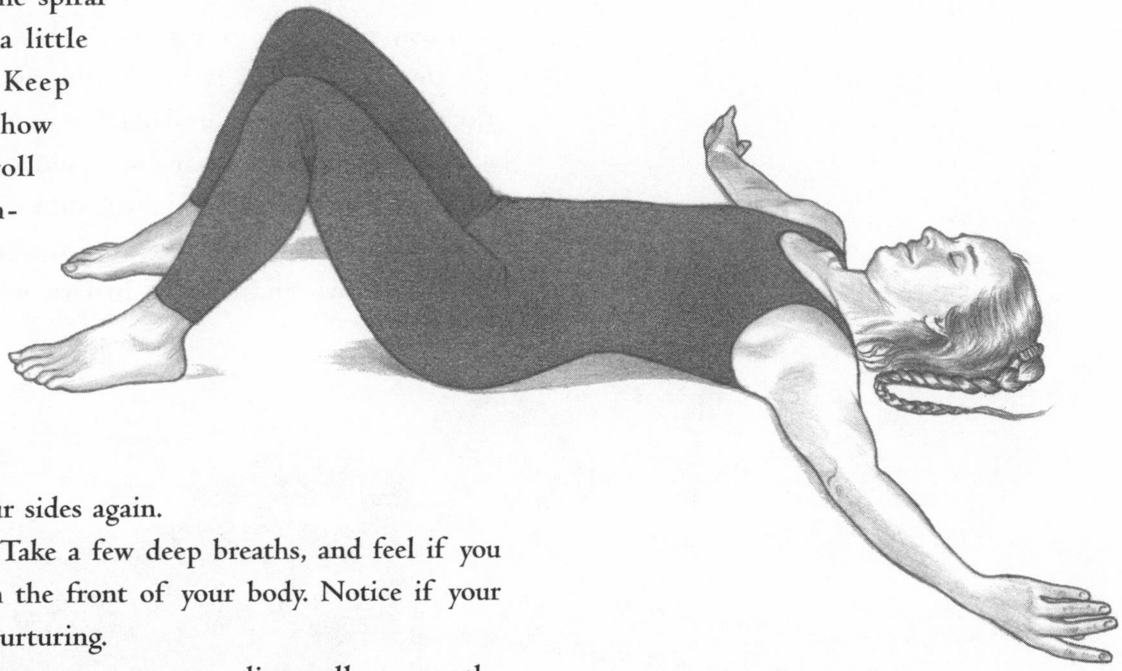

Now rest your arms at your sides again. Notice how your body feels. Take a few deep breaths, and feel if you have more breathing space in the front of your body. Notice if your breath feels easier and more nurturing.

Now let's focus on opening up more space diagonally across the front of your body. Once again, stretch your arms straight out from your shoulders in a T-formation. Rest your hands on the outside edges of your palms. Bring your knees up so that your feet are flat on the floor. Put your feet a comfortable distance apart and a comfortable distance from your buttocks.

Slowly roll one arm down the floor as your other arm rolls up the floor, then reverse. Remember, roll them like logs—don't let them slide. As the palm of one hand touches the floor, the back of the other hand will touch the floor. Then go back in the opposite direction. Re-

FIGURE 17.

Rolling One Arm Up the Floor as the Other Arm Rolls Down the Floor

peat this sequence slowly several times until you have the feel of it. You may now begin to expand the range of motion. Roll one arm up the floor as much as is comfortable as the other arm rolls down the floor through its comfortable range of motion. Keep the motion going without pausing at the transition point.

As your arms roll in opposite directions, you may notice that your head wants to roll slightly toward the arm that's rolling up the floor. This is normal and natural. In fact, we want to encourage it. So let

FIGURE 18.

Your Head Rolls Toward the Arm Rolling Up the Floor

your head roll as far as is comfortable toward the arm that's
rolling up the floor, then let
it roll the other direction
as you reverse the direc-
tion of your arms. Prac-
tice this a few times to
get the feel of it.

Now let's complete the
movement by involving the lower part of
your body. Let your knees drop gently over toward
the side where your arm is rolling *down* the floor, then as your
arms reverse directions, let your knees drop over toward the other side.
Keep your feet on the floor. The movement is designed to be slow and
gentle, more like a meditation than exercise. If you find yourself
straining, make a smaller movement or stop and rest.

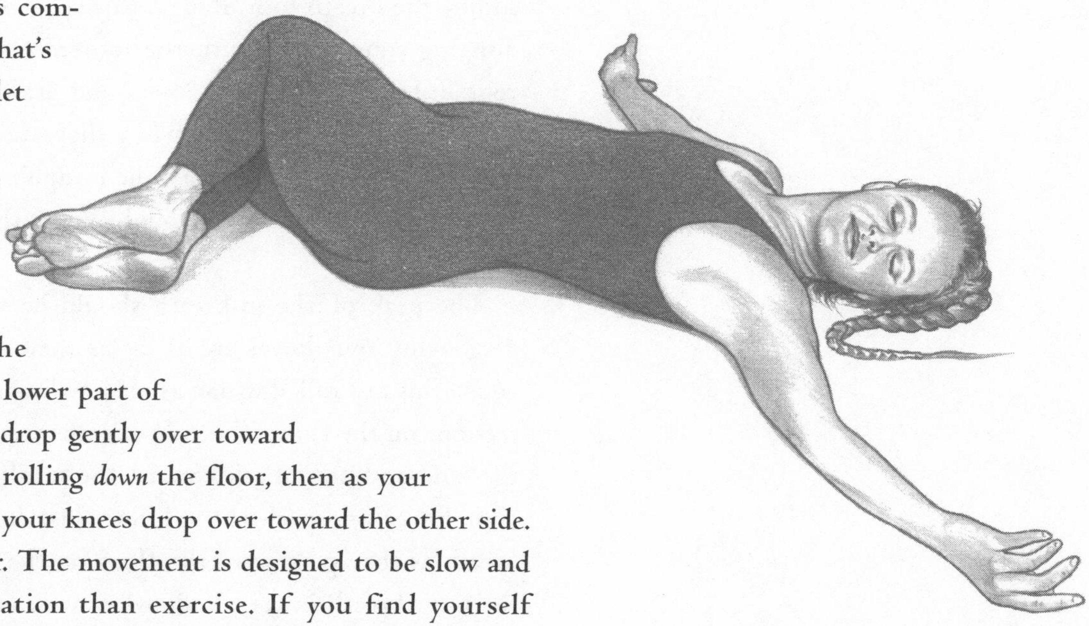

Your head is now rolling in the opposite direction from the side
your knees are dropping toward. Feel how this movement gives you a
stretch through your entire spine. Do this movement slowly and gently
about ten times. Make it one continuous movement, without pausing at
any point during it.

We call this movement the Spiral, because it puts spirals through
major joints of the body. The Spiral is ideal for opening the joints to
allow more energy to flow through. It also stretches the front of your
body so that you can get a larger breath.

We can make this beautiful movement even more exquisite by

FIGURE 19.

*The Full Spiral Movement Opens Space for Your
Body to Breathe Deeply*

adding the breath to it. Repeat this sequence ten to fifteen times, coordinating your breath with the movement in the following way. Start your in-breath when your knees and arms are at their midpoint. The midpoint of your knees is when they are crossing the center of your body, pointed at the ceiling. The midpoint of your arms is when they are straight out from your shoulders, neither moving up nor down the floor.

The peak of the in-breath should be when you are fully extended diagonally. Your knees are as far as they will go toward the floor, and your arms are rolled as far as they will comfortably go in opposite directions on the floor. Your out-breath starts as soon as your knees leave the side and start back toward the midline. The out-breath ends as your knees approach the midline, just in time to start another out-breath as they go toward the floor on the opposite side. You will have the most breath in your body when your body is the most extended diagonally. You will have the least breath in your body at the midpoint.

(Pause for ten to fifteen breaths of practicing this sequence.)

Now we have three major body systems moving with your breath. You are rolling one arm down the floor as the other arm rolls up, and you're dropping your knees toward the side where your arm is rolling down. You're rolling your head opposite to where your knees are going. Your breathing is hitting the peak of the in-breath when your knees are to the side, and you are finishing your out-breath when your knees are approaching the midline. You are getting a full spinal stretch with each breath, and at the same time you are gently stretching the muscles across the front of your body. If you take careful notice, you can feel the muscles from your shoulder to deep in your groin opening up with each stretch and breath you take.

(Practice ten or twenty times until you are ready to take a break.)

When you feel ready for a rest, stretch your legs out on the floor, place your arms back at your sides, and rest. Now and then take a big breath into the center of your body, and feel if you notice any new breathing space. When you are finished with this lesson, resume your normal activities.

This completes Advanced Lesson One.

DISCUSSION

Do not be surprised if it takes you a while to master this practice. It involves some very subtle reprogramming of your nervous system. My recollection is that it took me about a month of daily practice to get it all in place. When I first heard some of Feldenkrais's directions twenty years ago, I thought he was speaking Martian instead of Israeli-accented English. I absolutely could not do some of the things he was talking about. But with practice they became possible, then easy, then bliss-producing. Stay with this lesson until you get that sense of blissful ease in your body when you practice.

Fine-Tuning Your Whole-Body Breath

Now we are ready to add a subtle and very powerful dimension to your breathing. As you have already seen, if there is a secret to conscious breathing, it is to relocate the center of breathing from the chest down into the lower abdomen. When you take a deep breath, you must learn to take it down deep in your center rather than up high in your chest. Later you can learn to center your breathing in your abdomen all day long. Surprisingly, the deeper you breathe in the center of your body, the more completely the rest of your body participates in each breath.

Once you learn whole-body breathing, one good breath in the center of your body can restore balance to your whole system. A healthy diaphragmatic breath takes you immediately out of fight-or-flight consciousness and toward the centered state that we are all seeking. At a purely physiological level, a healthy breath will actually balance the mixture of gases that determine whether you will feel on edge or relaxed. I have often been amazed at how quickly I am able to restore a calm and energized feeling inside myself by taking a few good breaths. Many times during the week I will catch myself holding my breath or being triggered into fight-or-flight breathing by some event. I usually notice it first by an alteration in my consciousness: My concentration gets foggy, and I feel an irritating edge of speediness in my chest. That is my cue to pause and take a few deep belly breaths. Within seconds the foggy feeling is gone, and I feel well again.

This lesson will assist you in centering your breath down deep in your body. It also will acquaint you with the exquisite way nature has designed your whole body to move with your breath.

INSTRUCTIONS

Begin this lesson by lying down on a firm, comfortable surface. Later in the lesson you will sit up, either on the floor or in a chair.

Lie down on your back. Bend your knees so that your feet are flat on the floor. Rest your arms at your sides.

Let's begin, as we have in other lessons, by taking a few slow, deep diaphragmatic breaths. Arch the small of your back as you breathe into your relaxed, rounded belly. When you breathe out, flatten the small of your back against the floor. Do this a few times to get it going in a smooth, easy manner.

Use your imagination to visualize the back of your pelvis as a clock-face. Let's say that noon is at the top of your pelvis, up near where it joins your spine. Six o'clock is at the bottom, down by your tailbone. As you breathe in and arch the small of your back, your pelvis rolls straight down toward six o'clock. When you breathe out fully and flatten your back, your pelvis rolls straight up the face of the clock toward noon. Take five or six slow breaths now, focusing on how smoothly you can roll up and down the face of the clock from noon to six, back and forth. Focus intently on the sensations in the back of your pelvis.

(Pause and practice for five or six breaths.)

Now come to rest in the very center of your clockface, just where the name of the clock might be. Let your breathing be relaxed and easy while you imagine a new dimension to the clock. Imagine that nine o'clock is on the right side of your pelvis and three o'clock is on the left. Let your knees fall gently and slightly from side to side. Do this very slowly, and feel that your pelvis rolls straight across the clockface horizontally, from three to nine and back. Do this a few times, focusing on making the movement very smooth.

(Pause to practice a few breaths.)

Return now to the basic whole-body breath, arching the small of your back as you breathe into your belly and flattening your back as you breathe out. Focus on the back of your pelvis, feeling it roll up and down the face of the clock, from noon to six and back up to noon. As you do this, shift your focus to the front of your pelvis, to a point halfway between your navel and the top of your pubic bone. If you like, you can measure and touch this area with your hand. Notice that if you keep this area very relaxed, your breathing will become easier and the movement of your pelvis will be smoother. Aim your in-breath for this center point between your navel and the top of your pubic bone.

Take ten to fifteen breaths now, focusing intently on the sensations of the back of your pelvis rolling up and down the floor.

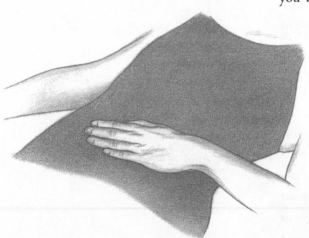

FIGURE 20.

Relaxing the Front of the Pelvis

Do your best to make this movement smooth. If you feel a glitchy place where there is raggedness or hesitation, go over it a few times even more slowly, as if you were ironing the wrinkles out of one of your favorite garments. Go for smoothness and ease of movement as you breathe.

(Pause.)

Take a rest now, leaving your pelvis in neutral, in the center of the clockface. Let your breathing go its own way for a moment or two.

(Pause.)

When you are ready to resume, exhale and roll your pelvis up to noon. Leave it there for a moment before you take your next in-breath. If you were going to roll in a clockwise direction around the outside edge of the clockface from noon to one to two to three, you would do this on the in-breath. If you were going to roll back counterclockwise from three back up to noon, you would do this on the out-breath. Go ahead now and breathe into your relaxed belly, rolling your pelvis around the clockface from noon to one to two to three. Use a slight movement of your knees to assist the rolling back and forth. Then on the out-breath, roll back around to noon. Continue this, focusing on the sensations of the movement. Feel any wrinkles, and go back over them to iron them out. Practice this movement for ten to fifteen breaths.

(Pause.)

Notice also that if you were going to roll around the edge of the clockface from noon down to six, you would also do this on the in-breath. Then, you would roll back around to noon on the out-breath. Go ahead and do this now half a dozen times. On the in-breath, roll clockwise around the clock to six, then counterclockwise back around to noon on the out-breath.

(Pause.)

Now take a big in-breath, rolling your pelvis around the edge of the clockface to six o'clock, and hold it there for a moment. If you were going to roll around clockwise through seven to eight to nine and on up to noon, you would do this on the out-breath. Go ahead now and breathe out as you roll around the edge of the clock from six on up past nine and on to noon. On the next in-breath, roll back down counterclockwise around the right side of the clockface to six, and as you breathe out, roll up the left side to noon. Make a few counterclockwise circles all the way around the clockface. Breathe in as you roll down the right side toward six, and breathe out as you roll up the left side toward noon. After you have made a few slow counterclockwise circles, go around clockwise a few times. Do the movements very slowly, focusing on the sensations. Go for smoothness and ease.

(Pause.)

When you have practiced the coordination of your breath and these subtle movements of your pelvis for thirty seconds or so, take a rest. Leave your pelvis in neutral, on the center of the clockface. If your legs are tired of their position, stretch them out on the floor. It might even feel good to shake them out a little.

(Pause and rest for a minute or so.)

We have been focusing our attention on the lower part of the body, particularly on the relationship between the pelvis and the breath. This relationship is an important one for our well-being. If you watch a healthy baby breathe, you will notice that its breath fills its relaxed belly fully and its pelvis moves with the breath, exactly in the way you were practicing earlier. When our fight-or-flight response is triggered, the breath freezes or goes up into the chest, and the pelvis freezes also. In other words, when we're scared, we lose our "healthy baby" breathing. These lessons are helping to restore your natural birthright, healthy breathing.

FIGURE 21.

Small Head-Lift

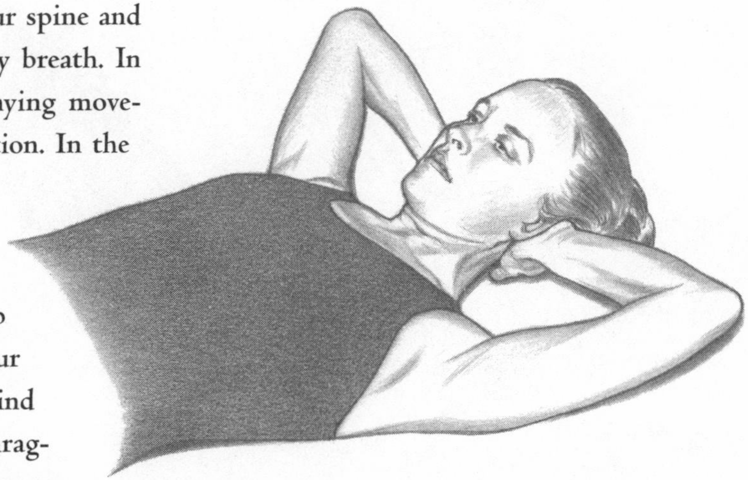

Now we will shift our attention to the other end of your spine and find out how the head is designed to move with a healthy breath. In these lessons we exaggerate the breath and its accompanying movements, making them bigger and making them in slow motion. In the learning phase of any new enterprise, especially one that involves reprogramming the nervous system, it is helpful to practice very slowly and deliberately.

When you are ready to continue, bring your knees up again so that your feet are flat on the floor. Interlace your fingers behind your head, making sure your fingers are behind your head, not your neck. Begin taking those slow diaphragmatic breaths we've been cultivating. As you breathe into your relaxed belly, arch the small of your back and roll your pelvis down the floor. As you breathe out, flatten the small of your back. Do this a few times, slowly and smoothly.

As you breathe out, lift your head a few inches off the floor with your hands. Let your hands do the work, keeping your neck muscles very relaxed. When you breathe in and arch your back, lower your head back to the floor. Repeat this movement, lifting your head with the out-breath and lowering it back to the floor on the in-breath. With your awareness, focus on both ends of your spine. Notice that your tailbone rolls down the floor toward its tip when you breathe in and lower your head, then up toward its connection with your spine when you breathe out and lift your head.

Now you have your spine moving through its full range of motion in coordination with your breath. This is exactly the way nature designed it and exactly the movement you will see in babies and in fetuses on ultrasound pictures. Practice this movement through ten to fifteen breath cycles, then stretch out your arms and legs and rest.

(Pause.)

When you are ready to continue, let's explore how this same pattern works as we move toward an upright position. Bring your knees up again, putting your feet flat on the floor.

FIGURE 22.

Use Your Hands for Balance

Raise your body up so that you are resting on your hands out behind you.

Take slow diaphragmatic breaths, using the same pelvic movement as you have practiced on the floor. Arch the small of your back slightly as you breathe into your rounded belly, then flatten the small of your back as you breathe out. Notice as you do this that you are rolling your tailbone toward its tip on the in-breath and toward your spine on the out-breath. After you've taken a few breaths like this, let's find out how the upper part of your body should move at the same time. When you breathe into your belly, arching the small of your back, look up with your head, pointing your chin toward the ceiling. When you breathe out, flattening the small of your back, tuck your chin down toward your chest. Breathe this way through ten to fifteen cycles. Go for ease and smoothness with this movement, and be sure to stay in your comfort zone.

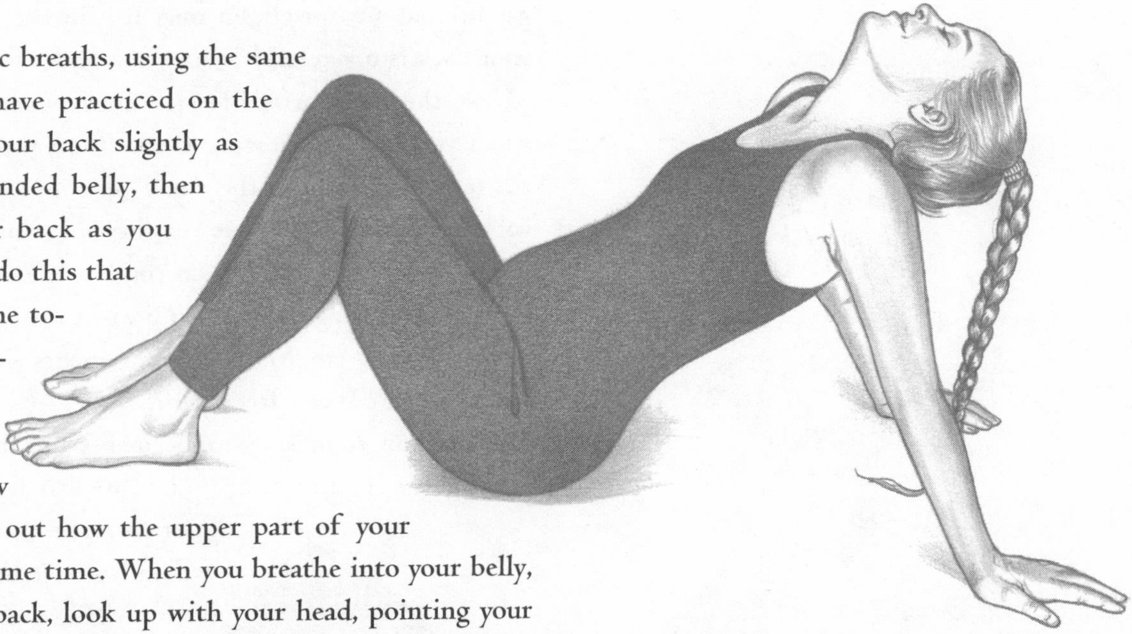

As you breathe, notice how you can open the upper portion of your chest as you breathe into your belly. At the same time as the breath goes down and into your belly, you look up toward the ceiling and make more space for it in your upper chest.

When you have finished ten to fifteen cycles, sit up straight and rest your arms at your sides or in your lap. If you feel comfortable sitting

FIGURE 23.

At the Peak of the In-Breath, Belly and Chest Are Opened Fully

on the floor, stay put. If you would feel more comfortable in a chair, get up and sit upright in one. If you use a chair, sit forward so that your back is not resting against the back of the chair.

Use the same principle and movements as you did a moment ago when you were supporting yourself on your hands. Breathe into your relaxed belly, arching the small of your back; breathe out, flattening your back. Let your pelvis tilt forward when you breathe in, backward when you breathe out. When you breathe in, tilt your head up as if to look at the ceiling. When you breathe out, tilt your head down as if to look into your lap. Make the movements slow and gentle. Breathe this way through ten to fifteen cycles.

Begin now to make the movements and the breath very subtle. Imagine you were in a meeting and wanted to breathe this way without calling attention to yourself. Do it so that no one would know it but you. Get the movements very refined and smooth. Take ten to fifteen of these refined breaths.

When you have finished, rest for a while, then resume your normal activities.

This completes Advanced Lesson Two.

FIGURE 24.

When the Out-Breath Is Fully Exhaled, the Back Is Rounded

Freeing the Breath Within the Breath

We have all felt the rhythms of the heartbeat and the breath, those two steady reminders of the preciousness of life. But many people do not know that there is a deeper, more fundamental rhythm that they can feel if they become sensitive to it. This rhythm is the movement of the cerebrospinal fluid as it pulses its lifegiving way from the brain down to the tip of the spine. As it flows along its spinal conduit, this fluid moves the core of the body in a slow pulsation. This movement is called the craniosacral rhythm, because it moves from the brain down the spine all the way to the sacrum with each of its pulsations. In older medical texts I have sometimes seen it called primary respiration.

The craniosacral rhythm is not talked about much in the conventional medical textbooks of today. Osteopathic physicians were once trained in the palpation of the rhythm and the use of its movement as a healing tool. Nowadays, many osteopaths have gravitated more toward standard allopathic medicine and away from the use of spinal manipulation and other techniques that were their province in the earlier part of the century. Unless you live in a major city, you may have to look hard to find a cranially trained osteopath today.

A gifted osteopathic physician, Dr. William Sutherland, first worked with the craniosacral rhythm over half a century ago. His students and colleagues, notably Dr. Viola Frymann, have carried on his tradition. My studies of breathing took me to seek training with Dr. Sutherland's disciples and finally to Dr. Frymann herself. I spent a brief but very productive time observing her work at her clinic in La Jolla, California.

In this lesson we will use awareness of the craniosacral rhythm to open up deeper space in the body in which breathing can occur. We will not work with the craniosacral rhythm to diagnose or heal specific problems, although I have seen gifted doctors like Viola Frymann do both with an ease and speed that bordered on the miraculous. To share an example with you, one of the doctor's specialties is distressed babies. A frantic mother would bring in a colicky baby with labored breathing and a heart-rending wail. Dr. Frymann would take the baby and work with its craniosacral rhythm, using her sensitive hands and five decades of experience. Often within a few minutes the baby's breathing would smooth out, and the anguished cries would be replaced by peaceful sleep. A very different mother would take the baby and leave the office. I was deeply moved and began experimenting with my own craniosacral rhythm as a way of improving my breathing. As you will probably see in this lesson, a small amount of attention to this subtle rhythm will bring you a noticeable improvement in the ease of your breathing.

INSTRUCTIONS

Lie down on your back on a comfortable and firm surface. A carpeted floor will work perfectly; a bed would be too soft for some of the movements to come later. Stretch your legs out, and rest your arms at your sides. The craniosacral rhythm is subtle; you must be patient with yourself in learning to feel it. Please do not think any less of

yourself if it takes you a while to get it isolated. At my first training workshop I got agitated because I was one of the last people
in the room to "find" it. Save yourself aggra-
vation by granting yourself plenty of space
to learn it. It's a little bit like learning to
ride a bike. One second you can't, and the next
second you can.

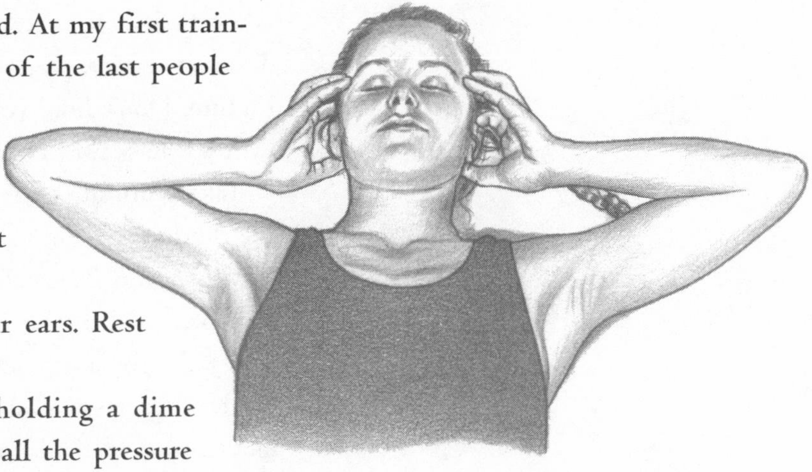

Place your fingertips lightly just above your ears. Rest
your arms on the floor so they won't get tired.

Use a very light touch. Imagine you are holding a dime
against your head with your fingertips. That's all the pressure
you need for this activity. Just "listen" with your fingertips for a
moment. You may be able to feel the pulse of your heartbeat here in
your head. As you tune in with your fingertips to your head, notice
something else quite interesting. Take a few deep breaths and see if
you feel your head expand when you breathe in. In fact, your whole
body expands slightly with the in-breath and contracts with the out-
breath. This swelling of the body with the in-breath can be measured
easily with sensitive scientific equipment, although it is not so easy to
feel with your fingers. Perhaps you can feel it, though, if you tune in
sensitively with your fingertips.

Now, to the craniosacral rhythm. Take a big breath and hold it for
ten or fifteen seconds. While your breath is held, see if you can feel a
slow and gentle widening and narrowing of the head. With your breath
rhythm out of the way, because your breath is held, you are more likely
to be able to feel the rhythm. Each cycle of the craniosacral rhythm

FIGURE 25.

Tuning In to the Craniosacral Rhythm

takes three or four seconds to swell and three or four seconds to recede. This is the average, although individuals may vary in the speed of their rhythm. Don't hold your breath to the point of discomfort. Rest for a little while between breath-holdings.

Take a minute or two to work with this practice until you can feel the rhythm.

When you have felt the rhythm and can distinguish it from your heartbeat and breath rhythm, take a rest. Stretch your arms down to your sides for a moment. While you are resting, touch your tongue to the roof of your mouth. Feel with your tongue that the roof of your mouth is shaped like a dome. Place your tongue in the center of the dome. Use a very light pressure with your tongue—as if you were "listening" with it. In a moment you may notice that the dome of the roof of your mouth is in motion! It flattens slightly every three or four seconds, then rounds upward again over three to four seconds. What is causing this movement is our new-found friend, the craniosacral rhythm. There are many places you can feel its rhythm—from your tailbone up to the crown of your head, even down in your feet—but the roof of your mouth is one of the best places to tune in to it.

Now let's actually create more space for this rhythm to move in. Bring your knees up so that your feet are flat on the floor. Rest your arms at your sides. Recall our imaginary clockface from Advanced Lesson Two. Put your pelvis in neutral, resting on the center of the clockface. Use your heels to help rock your pelvis gently and rapidly—noon, six, noon, six. Keep playing with the rocking until it gets easy and you develop a rhythm. Use small movements, more like jiggling even than rocking. After twenty or thirty seconds of gentle rocking, you may notice that you suddenly want to take a big breath. Let this happen. Often when cerebrospinal fluid has more space to move in, it calls for a deeper breath. Other than taking these big breaths when you feel them come up spontaneously, do not try to breathe in any particular way.

Keep rocking as long as it's comfortable, perhaps a minute or two. Do your best to keep your body very relaxed. The more you relax, the easier the rocking is. Notice particularly how relaxing your neck makes the rocking easier. After a minute or two, take a break and stretch your legs out on the floor. Notice if you feel any new sensations or feelings in your body.

(Pause and rest for a minute or so.)

When you are ready to resume, keep your legs stretched out straight and your arms relaxed at your sides. Let your attention go to your feet. Keeping your heels on the floor and using them as the fulcrum, begin rapidly to flex and extend your feet. By doing this you will rock your pelvis as you did earlier, although it will feel different now because of the position of your legs. Specifically, there will not be as much rocking room as before; the rocking will be smaller and more subtle. It is more of a jiggling of your pelvis than a rocking. Notice that if you can relax all your muscles, particularly your neck muscles, the rocking will be easier and smoother. After rocking for twenty or thirty seconds, you may notice that your body wants to take a deep breath. Whenever this happens, cooperate with it and take a big breath. Otherwise, do not try to breathe in any particular way.

Keep this rocking going for as long as it's comfortable and fun. After a couple of minutes, take a break and rest. During your break, tune in to your body sensations. See if you notice any new feelings in your body. Many people feel a tingling or streaming sensation after a few minutes of this movement.

After resting, touch above your ears with your fingertips. Now and then hold your breath and feel the craniosacral rhythm making your head swell and contract every three seconds or so. Do you feel it more strongly now? Is the rhythm more prominent? Smoother? Often, the rocking you have been doing creates more space for the rhythm, letting it come through in a more palpable way. If you can feel this, fine. If not, don't worry. Just enjoy your sensations and rest for a little while. When you are ready, resume your normal activities.

This completes Advanced Lesson Three.

DISCUSSION

I hope you have enjoyed learning to feel this subtle and perhaps unfamiliar rhythm. To me, learning something I didn't know about myself or human beings in general is one of the joys of life. Once I was spending an evening with one of my closest friends, a physician classically trained at Yale, Stanford, and other citadels of Western medicine. The subject of the craniosacral rhythm came up, and my friend flatly denied that there was any such thing. "If there was, I would've heard of it," was the (arguably arrogant) way he put it. Eager to score a "gotcha" on him, I had him lie down on the floor and guided him through an abbreviated form of the lesson you just finished. I watched him go from smug skepticism to wonder and delight. "I like having a new rhythm that I didn't know about," he said, gracefully going down to intellectual defeat.

In my own life I use this lesson primarily as a centering technique. If I am feeling the need for a deep connection with myself, I can think of no more reliable way to generate it. Learning to listen to the deepest rhythm of our bodies returns us to a primal connection with ourselves. Geologists tell us that the earth itself breathes like this, in slow pulsations of expansion and contraction. By tuning in to our own deep rhythm of expansion and contraction, we may find an enhanced connection with the rhythms around us. Cosmology aside, it feels great.

ADVANCED LESSON FOUR

Breathing into a Profound State of Relaxation

I wish I could relive an exquisite experience I had some years ago that reveals the deep power of this lesson. The scene was a hotel ballroom in Kansas City, where approximately one hundred and fifty people had gathered to experience the technique we are about to explore. As we began, there was the usual rattle and hum of a large group of people getting onto one another's wavelength. Within the first five minutes of this lesson, though, a hush fell over the participants as they began to experience the deep, sweet state of bliss that the technique can bring about. But it didn't stop there. Over the next twenty to thirty minutes a feeling filled the room that was part reverence, part awe. Later, one of the participants said that it was as if "we'd all gone to heaven together and come back." At the end of the lesson no one even wanted to talk, so profoundly altered were they. They quietly stood up, smiled and murmured their thanks, and floated out of the room.

While I cannot guarantee you a similar experience, I can tell you that I have yet to see this technique fail to move people who took the time to appreciate it.

INSTRUCTIONS

Lie down on your back on a comfortable surface. Stretch your legs out with your feet about eighteen inches apart, and rest your arms at your sides.

During this lesson you will be tensing and letting go in one part of your body while breathing very slowly and consciously. It is important to let your breathing and the rest of your body be very relaxed as you consciously tense each specific part.

Let's begin. Take the longest, slowest in-breath you can, keeping your body very relaxed. Take a long, slow out-breath, all the way to the last tiny bit of the breath. Then pause and wait for the next in-breath to surprise you. In other words, pause after the out-breath and wait until your body says "time to breathe." It might be a second, or it might be ten or fifteen seconds. Then when the in-breath comes, take another long, slow in-breath all the way to the top of your breath. Don't hold at the top—let the top melt right into the out-breath. Take a long, slow out-breath and pause. Wait until your body surprises you with its spontaneous in-breath. Use what you have learned about breathing deeply into your abdomen to get the breath down into the center of your body.

Keep repeating this sequence now for a minute or two: Long in-breath melting into a long out-breath, then pause after the out-breath and wait for your body to surprise you with its next in-breath.

(Pause and practice for a minute or two.)

Now let's add a new dimension to your breathing. As you take your long, slow in-breath, make a fist with your right hand. Stay in the comfort zone, but tighten your fist enough so that you know that it's tense. Keep the rest of your body and your breathing very relaxed; just focus all your tension on that right fist. On the out-breath, let go of the tension in your right hand. Let it all go, and keep letting go throughout your long out-breath. Then pause after the out-breath and wait for your next in-breath to surprise you. When it does, tense your right fist again all the way through the in-breath to the top, then let go of the tension throughout the out-breath.

On your next in-breath, tense your right fist and arm, all the way up to your shoulder. Hold the tension throughout your long, slow in-breath, keeping the rest of your body completely relaxed. Let go of the tension on the out-breath, continuing to let go more and more all the way to the end of the out-breath. Pause and wait for the next in-breath. Repeat the sequence with your right hand and arm.

Now relax and rest from the conscious tensing of your right hand and arm. Continue your breathing as before. Long, slow in-breath melting into long, slow out-breath, then pause and wait for the in-breath when your body calls for it. As you breathe, tune in to the sensations in your right arm, and compare those sensations to your left arm. Notice any differences you feel. There are no right or wrong answers here; just notice the sensations you feel in your two arms.

Now let's repeat the sequence as before, only this time with your left arm. Make a fist and tense it on your long, slow in-breath, then let go of the tension all the way through the out-breath. Pause at the end of the out-breath, tensing your left fist again only when you are surprised by the in-breath. After two or three cycles, add your left arm to the sequence, tensing both hand and arm with the in-breath. Repeat this pattern two or three times.

Now, rest and relax your whole body. Continue your breathing as before, but simply feel and listen to your body sensations. Compare your right arm to your left arm. Notice any differences and similarities.

When you are ready to resume, tense both hands and arms on the in-breath. Let go of the tension on the out-breath, then wait for the in-breath to come when your body calls for it. Do several cycles with both arms.

Again, pause and rest from tensing for a minute or two. Feel and listen to your body sensations.

Now let's move to your lower body. As you tense your right leg on the in-breath, keep the rest of your body very relaxed and let your breathing be very long and smooth. Relax the tension on the out-breath. When the last little bit of breath is gone, pause and wait for the in-breath. When it comes, tense your right leg again. Repeat this sequence a few more times.

Add your right hip and buttock to the tension pattern. Tense leg, hip, and buttock on the in-breath, and let them go on the out-breath. Use the longest, slowest breaths you comfortably can.

Pause and rest for a minute or two. Tune in to the sensations in your right leg. Compare the sensations to those in your left leg. Notice any differences and similarities.

Do the sequence with your left leg. Start with the leg only, then extend the tension pattern to your left hip and buttock. Repeat it several times.

Rest and listen to your sensations. Compare the sensations in your left leg to those in your right.

Now, tense your right and left legs together, all the way up into your hips and buttocks. Tense all the way with the in-breath, then let go throughout a long, slow out-breath. Pause until the in-breath surprises you, then do the tension pattern again. Repeat the sequence several times.

Finally, tense your hands, arms, and legs at the same time. Tighten your fists and arms, legs and buttocks, as you breathe slowly in. Melt right into the out-breath and simultaneously let go of the tension in your arms and legs. Keep letting go all the way until there is no more air, then pause and wait for the in-breath. Repeat the sequence several times.

Rest now and take your mind off your breath. Let your body breathe however it wants to breathe. Tune in to your whole-body sensations. Notice what you feel in your body and your mind.

Rest and enjoy your body sensations for as long as you want. When you feel finished, take as much time as you need to get to your feet, then resume your normal activities.

This completes Advanced Lesson Four.

Generating a Deep Experience of Streaming Energy

In this lesson we use conscious breathing to raise your positive-energy thermostat. Many of us have that thermostat set far too low. We struggle to prove we're okay, rather than relaxing into our magnificence. To make matters worse, many of us have self-sabotage mechanisms that come into play when our energy gets too high. We feel close to a loved one, then start an argument. We get a buzz working out at the gym, then go for the triple-cheese baconburger and feel miserable the rest of the evening. When I first started as a therapist twenty-five years ago, I thought that people created negativity because they felt bad. Now, with many years' experience, I see that it is often when things are beginning to go well that we mess up. I think it is because we do not have as much experience with feeling good, with things going well. Being happy, organically high, and successful is unfamiliar territory. When we stray into it, we often bring ourselves back into the familiar world of suffering and restriction.

So it behooves us to find ways of gently increasing our ability to handle positive energy. This lesson provides a way of doing it that is simple and feels delicious. I use it often myself, perhaps once a week, because it gives me a lift into new dimensions every time I do it.

To breathe fully and freely is to be powerfully inspired, sensually aroused, and sexually fulfilled as body, mind, and spirit.
—MICHAEL SKY

INSTRUCTIONS

Lie down on your back on a comfortable surface. There is little movement with this lesson, so you won't need much space around you. Rest comfortably with your legs stretched out and your arms at your sides. Throughout this lesson, do your best to keep the periphery of your body, your arms and legs, very relaxed.

We are going to alternate between periods of deep, relaxed breathing and periods of rest. In the early stages of the lesson you will take twelve deep, relaxed breaths, then rest for a minute or so. Then you will take twelve more deep breaths and rest again. During these rest times just let your breathing go at its own pace; take your mind off your breathing, and put your attention on your internal body sensations. As the lesson progresses we will move from taking twelve breaths to taking twenty-one breaths at a time. After years of experimentation I have found that cycles of twelve breaths at first, expanding to cycles of twenty-one later, provide the highest-quality experience.

Now let's begin. Breathing through your nose and into your relaxed abdomen, take twelve deep, full breaths in and out. Count them on your fingers or in your mind. Keep the breaths connected; do not pause at the end of the in-breath or the out-breath. Let one melt into the other. A suggested rhythm is three seconds for your in-breath, three seconds for your out-breath. You can look at a watch until you get the feel of what a three-second breath feels like.

When you reach twelve, relax and rest. Tune in to your inner body sensations. Notice what you feel. Particularly, notice if you feel any of the following sensations: tingling, buzzing, or humming feelings in your body. Notice also the quality of light in your mind. Notice if it is all light, or a combination of dark and light, or all dark. There are no right or wrong answers. Just notice what you notice. As the lesson progresses, you may notice more light in your mind and more of a combination of tingling, buzzing, and humming in your body. We'll call this latter complex of sensations streaming energy.

The gradual build-up of streaming energy is actually resetting your positive-energy thermostat higher, so it is an entirely positive experience. If you feel anything unpleasant as you practice this technique—such as tension or any uncomfortable feeling—pause from the deeper breathing and rest until the uncomfortable sensation passes. Never push into or push through any unpleasant feelings. Just pause and rest until they pass. In fact, one of the teachings you can take away from this lesson is how to stop and rest when you are feeling good. Often we wait to rest until we feel uncomfortable. Why not cultivate the skill of resting when we are feeling great?

After a minute or so of resting and noticing, begin taking those deep, full breaths through your nose and in and out of your relaxed abdomen. Take twelve of them, counting as you go.

After twelve deep breaths, rest and notice your body sensations. Do you feel any streaming energy—tingling, buzzing, or humming—in your body? Many people notice it first in their hands and arms. Tune in to the quality of light in your mind. Is it all light? Is it dark? Or a combination of light and dark? Just notice.

After a minute or so of rest, take twelve more deep, full breaths into your relaxed abdomen. When you reach twelve breaths, rest and let your breathing come and go as it pleases. Feel any streaming energy in your body, and notice the quality of light in your mind.

After a minute or so of rest, begin a longer breathing cycle. This time, take twenty-one deep, full breaths into your relaxed abdomen. Keep your body very relaxed as you breathe in and out through your nose. When you get to twenty-one, rest and relax. As you pause, tune in to your body sensations. Notice any streaming energy you feel. Notice the quality of light in your mind. Is it different now from when you started? Relax and let yourself go into the sensations.

After you have rested with your sensations a minute or two, return to your deep breathing. Take twenty-one deep, full breaths through your nose into your relaxed abdomen. Keep your arms and legs very still and relaxed as you breathe.

When you have taken your twenty-one breaths, rest and relax for a minute or two. While resting, tune in to any sensations of streaming energy you may feel. Notice also the quality of light in your mind. Enjoy the sensations in your body and the light in your mind.

Take a third and final deep-breathing cycle of twenty-one breaths. When you are finished, rest and enjoy the sensations in your body for as long as you want. When you are ready, come back upright slowly to avoid feeling dizzy.

This completes Advanced Lesson Five.

DISCUSSION

As you become more familiar with this lesson, you can extend your practice by taking more cycles of twenty-one breaths. Please remember, though, that this practice only works well if you stay in the comfort zone. Do not ever push into any negativity. If you should uncover any tension or unpleasant sensations of any kind during the practice, the way to handle them is by resting until they pass. Shift to quiet breathing if anything unpleasant comes up, resuming a deep-breathing cycle only when you feel completely at ease again.

I have done this practice forty-five minutes to an hour at a time, with very strong feelings of bliss coursing through my body. The secret to generating these deep bliss sensations is to "surf" on the upper edge of your positive energy, being very mindful of any negative sensations that creep in. When you sense the slightest possibility of negativity, shift to a rest cycle until you feel completely positive again.

CHAPTER 5

The Short Form

The Ten-Minute Daily Breathing Program

IF YOU ARE LIKE ME, YOU ARE PROBABLY TOO BUSY to do all the lessons every day. I often do the full Conscious Breathing Program once a week, taking an hour or so to enjoy both the Foundation and Advanced Lessons. But for everyday use, I recommend the short form that follows. In this section you will learn the Daily Breathing Program that I do every day of my life. My wife, Kathlyn, and I have now taught it to several thousand trainees, with many refinements and modifications along the way. Our current version contains what we feel to be the absolute essentials. I personally think any human being could benefit from doing it every day.

The program is designed to give you a deep sense of centeredness, a base of healthy breathing from which to operate as your day goes along. My recommendation is to do this program regularly every morning. I sometimes do it in the evening, too, but I seldom miss a morning. Kathlyn and I have gathered data from several hundred of our students who have been practicing the program daily for at least a year. The most commonly reported benefit is a stable supply of energy throughout the day. Other typical benefits include deeper and more restful sleep, greater calm, disappearance of physical complaints such as pain and tension, easing of menstrual difficulties, and sharper concentration.

Think of this program as preventive maintenance. Just as a little daily attention to toothbrushing can prevent painful and dramatic occurrences later, so it is with breathing. Make tiny daily improvements in this crucial part of your life, and you will likely be amazed at the results.

The Daily Breathing Program assembles components with which you are already familiar from the Foundation and Advanced Lessons.

INSTRUCTIONS

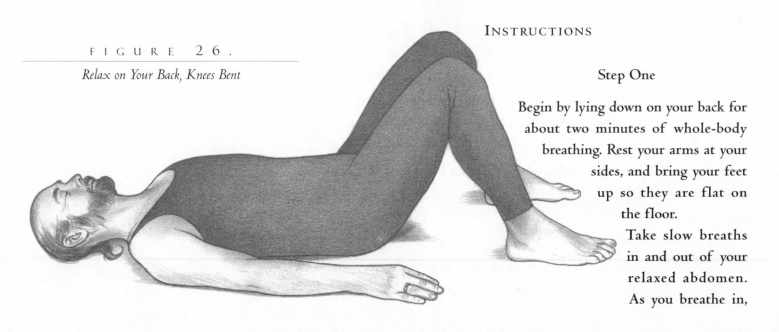

FIGURE 26.

Relax on Your Back, Knees Bent

Step One

Begin by lying down on your back for about two minutes of whole-body breathing. Rest your arms at your sides, and bring your feet up so they are flat on the floor.

Take slow breaths in and out of your relaxed abdomen. As you breathe in, arch the small of your back gently, then flatten it against the floor on the out-breath. Make your movements gentle and easy, focusing on the sensations of your spine flexing with your breath.

Practice for two minutes.

After two minutes, stretch out your legs and rest for a moment.

Step Two

Now we will do about two minutes of the spiral movements you learned in Advanced Lesson One.

Lie on your back. Bring your legs up so that your feet are flat on the floor. Stretch your arms out in a T-formation.

Now slowly begin the spiral movements.

Roll one arm up the floor as the other rolls down. Roll them slowly back and forth. Let your knees drop over toward the side where your arm is rolling down. Let your head turn opposite to the direction your knees are going. When you get this movement smooth and coordinated, add your breathing to it. Breathe in and expand your belly as your knees near the

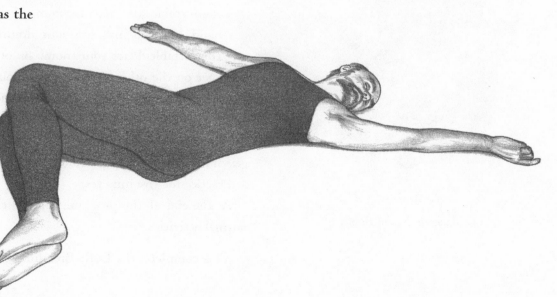

FIGURE 27.

The Spiral Movement

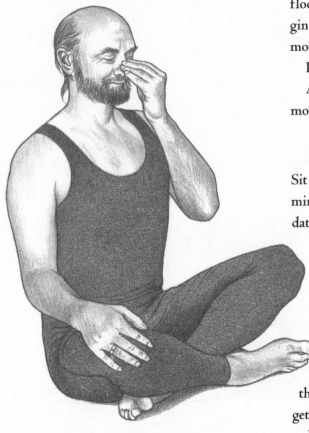

FIGURE 28.

Alternate-Nostril Breathing

floor, then breathe out as your knees lift toward the midpoint. Then begin another in-breath as your knees drop to the other side. Do the movements and the breathing very slowly, focusing on your sensations.

Practice for two minutes.

After your practice, stretch out your legs and rest for a few moments.

Step Three

Sit upright in a chair or on a cushion. You are now going to do five minutes of alternate-nostril breathing, just as you learned in Foundation Lesson Three.

You may close your eyes or keep them open, whichever is more comfortable for you. I recommend that you use your nondominant hand, but you may use your dominant hand if that feels most comfortable. Place your thumb on one nostril and your middle finger on the other. Breathe slowly out one nostril and back in that same nostril. Close that nostril and breathe out and in the other nostril. Always make your switch after the in-breath. Alternate in this fashion for five minutes. You may find that the breath slows and gets more subtle as you go along. Allow it to change as it wants.

Practice for five minutes.

At the end of the program, you can rest for a while or resume your normal activities.

This completes the Daily Breathing Program.

PART III

Conscious Breathing for Special Concerns

Introduction to Part III

I HAVE HAD THE OPPORTUNITY TO TEST THE EFFECTIVENESS OF CON-
scious breathing techniques with several thousand clients with a wide
variety of problems. In the realm of mental health, I have been very
impressed by the way these techniques work with such common clinical
problems as anxiety and depression, as well as coping with the everyday
stresses and tensions of life. One of the greatest benefits of conscious
breathing is in release from the traumas and wounds of the past. Conscious breathing is of great value in working with problems that lie on the
border between mental and physical health, such as asthma, headache, and
spastic colon. In this section I will describe how to use breathing for some
of these special problem areas. The reader is also referred to the section
on breathing in the book my wife, Kathlyn, and I wrote on our body-centered therapy approach, *At the Speed of Life*.

My suggestions will be based mainly on my own experience and on
that of some of my closest colleagues. In other words, I will rely on clinical experiences rather than empirical research. In a book such as this,
where I am keenly interested in the practical application of the tech-

niques, there is not enough room to present the reams of research data on breathing as a clinical tool. However, please do not think that the research literature does not exist or has been ignored. There is solid research-based support for the use of breathing with all the problems I mention. If you are interested, I highly recommend a trip through the research literature on breathing. In preparing to write this book, I spent many happy hours in the University of Colorado library accessing the research on the new CD-ROM version of Psychological Abstracts and on Med-Line. My notes indicate that I accessed 302 articles in Psychological Abstracts and many others on Med-Line. So far, I have turned up about a thousand research papers that relate to the subject with which we are concerned.

As I tapped into this rich vein of research on breathing, my amazement grew: Given what we know about this subject, why has it been so roundly ignored by the orthodoxy of both medicine and psychology? I don't know the answer to that question. I can, however, point to some encouraging developments. I sometimes go to the annual Biofeedback Society conference, usually held in my back yard at the Broadmoor Hotel in Colorado Springs. I have kept track over the years of the number of lectures, workshops, and papers given on the subject of breathing. There has been steady growth each year. In the last few years, there has also been a steady growth in the number of presentations on breathing at the American Medical Association's annual conference.

So there is cause for hope for those of us who know the power of conscious breathing to improve the quality of life. In Part III I will highlight several specific areas that broad segments of the population need to know about. Beginning with a generalized approach to trauma release, we will deal with asthma, addictions, and other problems of common concern. Where possible, I will include transcripts from therapy sessions, so that you can see how the techniques are integrated into actual practice.

CHAPTER 6

The Trauma Release

Healing Wounds in the Past and Present

O NE OF THE PRINCIPLES WE TEACH THE STUDENTS in our body-centered therapy training program is: Any trauma you can breathe through loses its grip on you. Here's why. Any animal freezes its breathing when a startle occurs. In nature "red in tooth and claw," there is great survival value in freezing into stillness. This primal wiring remains in our bodies today. I once was teaching a class when an explosion occurred that shook the building. There was a collective gasp as thirty people grabbed a breath. Later we laughed about it, because shortly before the explosion I had been lecturing on the fight-or-flight response.

When a trauma occurs, the breath is first held and then becomes short and shallow. So releasing a trauma from the body and mind is partly a result of getting the breath flowing again while the person consciously processes the feelings from the events that froze the breath in the first place.

Watch breath, soften belly, open heart, has become a wake-up call for mindfulness and mercy, which takes people beyond the mind-body of suffering into the deep peace of their healing.
—STEPHEN LEVINE

A second factor in trauma is communication. In the beginning of healing you may need to tell the story from the position of a victim or from total self-blame. The important first step is to communicate about the trauma any way you can. I recall a mugging victim screaming "I hate you, I hate you, I hate you!" perhaps fifty times during the course of a breathwork session. Others may turn their anger inward, saying "What did I do to deserve this?" Eventually, though, a shift will begin to occur toward resolution.

Another principle we use: Trauma has been released from the body when you can communicate about it in the same tone of voice you use to tell someone the time. This is not to be confused with the emotionally flat tone of denial; rather, it is the relaxed tone that means you are at peace with what you are saying. Some people stay in the grip of a trauma because they blame themselves in some way for what happened. Many others perpetuate the trauma by never getting beyond the perception of themselves as victims.

Ultimately, though, a middle ground can be found. Healing lies between the two extremes of "I am wrong" and "They are wrong." As people heal from traumas, they tend to regard the events with dispassion and compassion. They think: This is what happened, this is the meaning I made out of it, these are the feelings I carried away from it, these are the decisions I made as a result. Above all, the healing person focuses on what he or she can do now to end the influence of the trauma in present life.

The Informal, Immediate Stress-Release Technique

I think all human beings could benefit from knowing how to release minor traumas and stresses from the body as they are occurring and immediately after. There are many times in life when events rattle our nervous systems. On your way to work in the morning, you could see an accident, hear the blare of a loud horn, and hit a pothole, all in the same minute. Each of these events can trigger the startle response. When the startle response goes off, the old animal programming inside you says: Freeze your body movements and hold your breath until the danger passes.

Unlike our fellow animals, we humans tend to hold on to our startle responses. The power of the human brain to generalize works against us in the realm of trauma. An animal hears a loud noise, freezes, then relaxes again rather quickly. No more threat, no more tension. Human beings take much longer to let go after a startling event. If we are exposed to trauma frequently, or if we are exposed to a very large trauma even once, we can hold on to the startle in our bodies for years afterward.

Take, as one example, the issue of noise. Scientists tell us that the noise in cities has been increasing at the rate of about one decibel a year for the past twenty years. If you went into a situation where the noise level was twenty decibels higher than normal, you would probably cringe. But if you slowly adapted to it—learned to live with one decibel more a year—how would your body react? We can only guess, but my sense is that in today's urban environments, people have gradually learned to steel themselves in various ways in order to function. My general observation is that people in cities do not breathe as deeply as people in the country. Noise, pollution, and other factors contribute to the collectively held breath of civilization.

Since I live in a quiet corner of the world in Colorado, I have frequent opportunities to notice how I adapt to the stresses of urban life. I spend about half my time on the road, giving lectures and workshops, so nearly every week I leave quietude and fly into some urban area. Predictably I have trouble sleeping the first night, due to sirens, horns, and such, but by the second or third night my body has made some adjustment that allows me to rest. If I am gone for a few days, I notice a definite unwinding effect when I return to the quiet and clean air of home. My body even lets go of fluids when I return, as if the stresses of urban life had encouraged it to hold on to moisture at the cellular level.

When I am in the city, I find myself paying even more attention to my breathing than when I'm at home. The reason is that there are more shocks to my system in urban areas. When I receive a startle, even a mild one, I notice a change in my breathing. Walking to my publisher's office in New York City a few weeks ago, conscious breathing was on my mind because I was going to talk to my editor about this book's progress. I decided to pay extra attention to my breath.

In the first block I encountered a man jackhammering a chunk of pavement. I found myself gritting my teeth and cringing in response to the sound. I realized my breath was held high in my chest for about ten seconds as I walked past. Two blocks later a movie was being filmed, and I paused to watch for a moment. Fascinated by the actors, lights, and cameras, I caught myself holding my breath again. As I neared my destination in the Times Square area, a street person came along, bellowing and gesticulating with an upraised fist. I averted my eyes: Again I noticed a held breath.

The strategy I use in such situations is simple, but it works: I return my breathing to the center of my body as soon as I am aware that I am holding it or pumping it up into my chest. Both these signals let me know I have kicked into fight-or-flight breathing. Then it's time to take a big belly-breath and consciously use my breathing to re-center. Specifically, I take three deep breaths and change my body position.

Recall that animals tend to freeze their body movements when under threat. Changing your body position breaks up the frozen movements of the fight-or-flight reflex. Taking a few deep breaths gets the energy flowing inside you again. I use this technique every day. Even after working with my breathing for twenty years, I still find that I get triggered into fight-or-flight breathing on a regular basis. Most of the time it doesn't take a jackhammer to do it, either.

Just a moment ago I noticed that I held my breath for a second when Kathy, the director of our institute, popped in to tell me something I didn't really want to hear. How should she handle a person who was calling repeatedly to demand to talk to me or my wife? Most people who call are polite in their requests; they know we will call them back when we get an opportunity. A tiny minority—they seem to come out in force right after we appear on a talk show—are not polite. When Kathy was finished telling me about this latest phone caller, I noticed that my breath-holding was hiding a feeling of anger at being interrupted. I started to tell her I was angry that she had interrupted me, but then I realized that I had left my door open, a signal that I am free to anybody who wants to poke a head in. So I just took a deep breath, silently acknowledged my anger to myself, gave a few instructions, and asked Kathy to close the door on the way out.

This is an example of informal trauma release. Although this was not much of a trauma, these tiny moments, if not handled properly, can cause a great deal of trouble. Suppose I had not breathed through my anger and taken responsibility for it. A more complicated scenario might have unfolded. I might have snapped at an innocent person. Kathy would have probably been hurt and confused: After all, the door was open. I might have also carried away some undealt-with feelings from the situation, which would then have needed handling later. As it turned out, the situation was handled on the spot, and I felt fine within seconds. Half a minute later I was busy at work on my book again, breathing comfortably with my door closed.

The Formal Trauma-Release Technique

While most of the stresses of life can be breathed through on the spot, sometimes a difficult, shocking event can literally and metaphorically knock the breath out of us. For deeper traumas, a more formal technique is called for. My wife and I have used the following approach with survivors of such traumas as rape, accidental electrocution, combat wounds, and mugging.

We initially devised this technique to work with people with post-traumatic stress syndrome, particularly those with post-war and post-sexual-assault reactions. However, it works well with many kinds of difficulties, not just with more extreme traumas. I will take you through it here, step by step, so that you can see how and why it works.

The process includes two basic elements: communication and breathing. A third element, touch, can be added if the individual feels comfortable with being touched. We never use touch without permission. Although the touch used in this technique—fingertips on the forehead—

is nonthreatening to most people, there are those who cannot handle even this minimal amount of physical contact. The illustration shows the body positions for the technique using touch. If the therapist is not using touch, he or she simply sits by the person's side.

What follows is the transcript from part of a session where the client, BK, was releasing a trauma involving a physical and sexual assault. I have edited out certain identifying details, attempting to leave intact the key elements of the instructions.

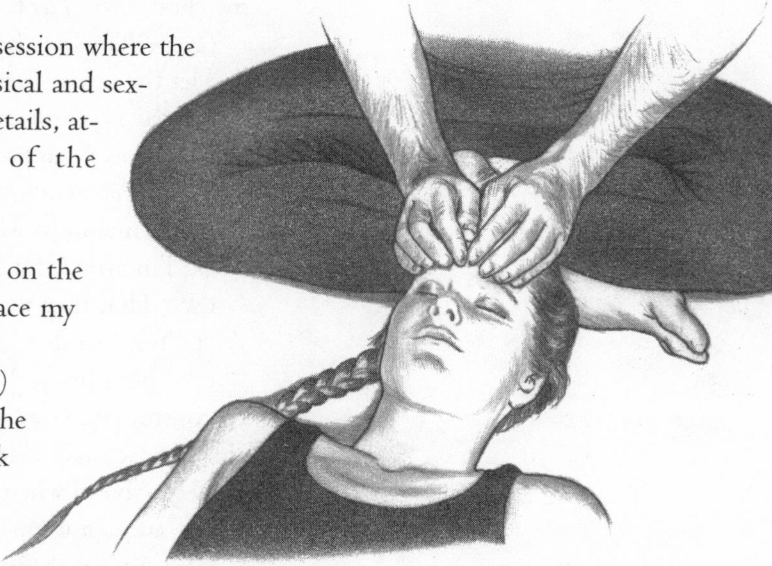

GAY: If you're ready, go ahead and lie down on the mat. I'm going to sit behind your head and place my hands on your forehead.

(She lies down and we take up our respective positions.)

What I'm going to do is to ask you to breathe in a slow, gentle way. From time to time I'll ask you to talk about whatever is going on for you, even if it seems to have nothing to do with the trauma. Meanwhile, I'll be resting my fingertips on your forehead, just above your eyebrows. We've found that these points on the forehead help people let go of things in a gentle way.

(Although I know little about Oriental medicine, several acupuncturists and Chinese doctors have told me that these points are well known in the East for facilitating trauma release. My own experience is that, in conjunction with breathing, these points really do speed up the gentle release of trauma. If my client expresses interest, I explain these details as best I can.)

BK: I'm scared.

GAY: Yes. Tune in to where you're noticing your fear.

FIGURE 29.

Body Position for the Trauma-Release Technique

BK: Mostly in my stomach.

GAY: What are you feeling? The actual sensations . . .

BK: Hmm. I guess some trembly feelings in my stomach. Up in my chest, too. (*Her breathing is very ragged and hesitant.*)

GAY: Okay. For the time being, let go of trying to control the fear and let the sensations be there.

(*At this suggestion her breathing shifts to a more relaxed rhythm. Often the breath is the most sensitive thing the therapist can watch to discover whether the client is flowing with her internal experience or trying to control it.*)

GAY: Tune in to what the fear is about. "I'm afraid that—"

BK: I'm afraid if I let go into all my feelings, I'll go crazy.

GAY: That they would overwhelm you.

BK: Yes, like that.

GAY: Mm-hmm. I notice that when you let go and stopped trying to control your fear, your breathing became deeper. Take a few deep, slow, conscious breaths down into your lower abdomen. Make your belly get round when you breathe in.

(*She takes a few deep breaths, and tears start to form in her eyes.*)

GAY: Accept those tears. Tell me about what you're feeling.

BK: I'm just remembering how kind my mother was when she came to visit me in the hospital. After the thing happened.

GAY: She was there for you.

BK: Yeah, and we've never gotten along very well since I've been on my own. I'm just sad we had to connect like that.

(*She cries unabashedly.*)

GAY: Take a few big breaths into the heart of the sadness.

(*She cries freely for about a minute, then subsides.*)

GAY: That's it. Just accept all that sadness, and let your breath be free like that.

BK: It's hard to accept.

GAY: I know. What is it about all of it—the whole experience—that's hardest to accept?

BK *(long pause):* I guess being powerless.

GAY: Yes, feeling powerless. And what about feeling powerless is the hardest thing to accept?

BK *(pause):* Losing control. Not being in control. Having somebody else have power over me.

(More sobs come.)

GAY: Breathe right into the center of all that feeling. Stay with it with your breath.

BK: I'm afraid if I really let go and feel it all, I'll be stuck with it, it'll always be there.

(She has very articulately put her finger on a key issue that keeps us stuck in our feelings. We think that if we feel them, they will always be with us. Paradoxically, the opposite is true. Feeling them completely clears them up; hiding them guarantees that they will always be with us.)

GAY: I understand. Check it out, though, inside yourself. Notice that it really works the other way around. If you let yourself feel it, it will stop bothering you. Feelings have a beginning, a middle, and an end, just like a thunderstorm. But if you try to look the other way and pretend they are not there, it becomes a problem.

(She took a big sigh at this point and got much more relaxed. I think of this as "the sigh of healthy acceptance." It's a sigh not of resignation, which has a different feel, but of simply accepting reality as it is. This move, of seeing and feeling something exactly as it is, is an important first step in change.)

BK: I get what you mean. *(Her breath is flowing deeply and slowly now.)* Just let it be the way it is. Let it go.

GAY: Yes, like that.

I have condensed this example considerably to highlight the generic healing moments, so please understand that it is not usually quite so straightforward. Often it takes many sessions to bring about resolution of a major trauma. The biggest problem people face in resolving traumas is not quitting when the tough feelings come up. In working with incest or rape survivors, for example, my wife and I have found that the truly tough feelings to resolve are usually those feelings that are not personally or socially acceptable. For most people, it is acceptable to feel scared and hurt, but other feelings are less often acknowledged. Survivors must face and deal with feelings like the urge for vengeance or their own sexual arousal during the trauma. These are very difficult feelings to accept in ourselves, and we tend to avoid dealing with them. But it is not until we accept all feelings and put them to rest that we can walk away from traumas healed and whole.

Communicating about the trauma to a listening, caring person speeds up the healing process. It is important to acknowledge feelings to ourselves: This in itself brings about a degree of healing. But to communicate about them clearly to another person, especially one who can encourage you to keep breathing, is a faster road to resolution.

CHAPTER 7

Using Breathwork in Recovery from Addictions

B Y NOW, THOUSANDS OF PAPERS AND BOOKS HAVE BEEN WRITTEN ON the treatment of alcoholism and other addictions. No one could possibly keep up with the explosion of information on this subject in recent years. Yet with all this research activity, it is puzzling how little work has been done on the use of body-centered techniques such as breathwork and movement therapy in healing addictions. A colleague, Christine Caldwell, recently searched the addictions literature of the past ten years for mentions of body-centered techniques. She found not a single book or article on the subject, although a few books mentioned it in passing.

This dearth of emphasis on the positive potential of the body is not surprising. After all, it is the hated body, with all its troublesome feelings, that the addict is attempting to poison. The body is the repository of pain, from which the addict seeks release. In addition, our culture tends to see the body as a utility vehicle, as Thomas Edison said, "to carry the head around." No wonder, then, that the addictions field is still virtually untouched by the power of body-centered therapies.

This is all about to change, however. I know of many works that will be coming into the journals and bookstores over the next year or two. Having had the opportunity to speak at addictions conferences every year since 1975, I have seen the field grow much more receptive to body-centered therapy. I believe that we are on the verge of a fresh new surge of information that will be of great help in treating addictions. The concepts and techniques of the body-centered therapies are tailor-made for the problems addicts face. It is only a matter of time before we see breathwork, movement therapy, and other body techniques regarded as necessary parts of the addictions-therapist's toolkit.

I have found the techniques in Part II of this book to be of great value in healing addictions. As I have mentioned, I am my own best customer. Breathwork was essential to me in healing three different addictions of my own. I discovered conscious breathing at a time when I weighed three hundred pounds and smoked two to three packs of Marlboros a day. I tackled my weight problem first, putting myself on a very restricted diet. For one month I ate nothing but fruits and vegetables, to my delight losing thirty pounds. Then, growing sick of the sight of vegetation of any kind, I went on a high-protein diet. The first two days, eating nothing but meat and fish washed down by eight glasses of water a day, I lost five pounds. From then on I alternated between the two plans, the nutritional equivalent of a manic-depressive. It worked, though, and I took off seventy-five pounds in six months. My diet coincided with some of my initial discoveries of conscious breathing, and thank goodness for that! Practically every day I was beset by powerful cravings for all the sugary, creamy substances that had been my staples for years. I found that I could make cravings disappear by deep, slow breathing right into the gnawing sensations.

Breathing was also helpful to me in another way. After losing about thirty-five pounds, I decided to reward myself with a huge ice cream sundae, drenched in hot fudge and topped with whipped cream. I was feeling great after my initial success, so naturally a celebration was called for. And what better way to celebrate than a sundae? Like most addicts, I was having a hard time handling success, so I chose a way of rewarding myself that guaranteed misery. After a month of healthy eating, the sundae hit my system like a toxic bombshell. I don't recall ever feeling sicker: Every cell in my body felt nauseous. Spontaneously I started deep breathing, and it got me through the nausea in half an hour or so.

To quit smoking, I used conscious breathing after taking an illicit detour. One of my friends, a trusting soul, had left a grocery bag full of marijuana in my safekeeping while he was away on a trip. I went cold turkey from cigarettes one fine day in 1971. On the first morning I tried to handle the strong cravings by furiously chewing big wads of gum. The cravings were a lot more intense by noon, and I felt that I was about to light up again. Suddenly a flash of genius struck: I would take a puff of marijuana when the cravings got bad. It would give me that feeling of smoke biting into my lungs that addicts, in their twisted way, love, and it would override the pain with some euphoria. Guess what? It worked. After dipping into the grocery bag a few times, I forgot all about my cravings for tobacco. But you can probably guess the down side of this innovative treatment program.

Within three days I had completely licked the urge to smoke tobacco. All that remained, the tiny problem that marred my program, was a powerful urge to smoke marijuana all the time. The level of my friend's grocery bag was dropping embarrassingly, and I found myself rolling a chubby one before my feet hit the floor in the morning. It had to stop, so I came up with another idea. Since I had started smoking in the womb (my mother was a heavy smoker throughout her life until it finally killed her), I decided that water should play a role in my healing process. Water and breath would be my cures. So every morning I jumped out of bed and forced myself to trot over to the Stanford pool. Never a graceful swimmer, I would thrash wildly up and down the lanes for an hour until I got an oxygen buzz. In other words, I found an organic way of getting high.

These two techniques—breathing through cravings and using breath to reach an organic high—became the mainstays of the way I work with alcoholics and other addicts. The addict needs to learn how to feel good with no negative side effects. After all, these are people who have learned to use a toxic chemical to feel good while simultaneously killing themselves. Their body-priorities and values are upside down. To learn to use self-administered doses of oxygen to feel good: This simple thing is for them a very important lesson.

Let me walk you through a recent experience I had helping someone stop smoking. Melanie is a woman in her mid-thirties who is very successful in her field but not very skilled in the area of relationships. She consulted me about this and related problems, and I told her she would have to stop smoking before I would work with her. I pointed out that the addiction was a major way of keeping men distant, especially the healthier types of men she was becoming interested in. I have also found that therapy is not particularly useful until after a person stops smoking. They cannot get to their deeper issues while they are wrestling with the addiction. I especially will not do breathwork with smokers until after they quit. I have found that increased oxygenation drives the toxins deeper inside; they often get a horrendous cold after a breathing session. I begin working with them right after they quit, however, and the new wave of vitality they bring into their bodies helps them forget the cigarettes.

I made a plan with Melanie for her to quit on a specific night at midnight. After ascertaining that she had not smoked the next morning, I took her through all three of the Foundation Lessons. We stayed with the exercises until her cheeks began to pinken, a sign to me that fresh energy was penetrating the cells. Smokers' skin takes on a yellow or gray cast as the result of oxygen deprivation; as soon as Melanie broke through to a healthier skin tone, I took her over to the mirror and showed her. I asked her to do the three Foundation Lessons three times each day, not stopping until she saw pink in her cheeks. When she got a craving for a cigarette, she was to do Foundation Lesson Three deeply and rapidly until the craving went away. This use of alternate-nostril breathing is very helpful to the recovering addict.

When I was in graduate school in the early seventies, the biofeedback revolution was just beginning. My friends and I spent many learning-filled hours wiring ourselves up to various machines used to monitor physiological responses. In clinical practice I have used biofeedback to help people with addictions develop a relationship with their bodies and learn to relax. The power of breathwork can be readily seen through the use of a machine like the electroencephalograph, or EEG, a device that measures the electrical patterns of the brain. It is not as widely used as other biofeedback equipment because it requires placing electrodes around the scalp. A glance at the tracings that the machine leaves shows the dominant areas of electrical activity throughout the cortex. When the person is in the grip of a craving, the brainwave picture on the EEG is very chaotic. There is little balance between the right and left hemispheres, and there is a tendency for the electrical activity to "bunch up" in certain areas.

Within a few seconds of alternate-nostril breathing, you can actually see coherence begin to appear on the screen. If the person can keep up the breathing for another minute or two, the EEG picture is remarkably different. Gone is the chaotic pattern, replaced by a unified field of balanced brain function. Left and right hemispheres come into harmony, seeming to share the load of brain activity.

Based on my experience working with perhaps three hundred people with various addictions, initially the most useful techniques are Foundation Lesson Three (Breathing for Mind/Body Integration) and Advanced Lesson Five (Generating a Deep Experience of Streaming Energy). These two techniques help the person through the short-term cravings right after the substance is withdrawn, and both of these techniques give the person a direct, immediate dose of positive energy. For the long term, however, all the lessons are useful. We eventually try to get all recovering addicts to do the short form, the Daily Breathing Program, on a regular basis. Those who do it uniformly report that the gradual daily introduction of more positive energy into their systems is of great benefit in redirecting their lives toward productivity rather than self-destruction.

CHAPTER 8

Conscious Breathing for Asthma and Other Respiratory Problems

ASTHMA IN ALL ITS FORMS AND LEVELS OF SEVERITY affects a great many people. Due to two factors, I have had the opportunity to work with a larger number of asthmatics than most psychologists ordinarily encounter. First, my interest in breathwork has brought many asthmatics to our institute, people who are seeking nonmedical treatments for their illness. Many of the drugs used to treat asthma have powerful side effects, so many asthmatics are highly motivated to find natural treatments for their problem. Second, there is a large treatment center for asthma and respiratory problems up the road from me in Denver. Some initial successes treating asthma during the 1970s brought me to their attention, which resulted in numerous referrals. I can say that few things in my professional career have given me more satisfaction than helping asthmatics learn to breathe effectively. To see a person, often a child, go from relying on powerful drugs to relying on his or her own natural powers of breathing—this is life at its finest for a healer.

Even staunchly conservative members of the medical community now tend to regard asthma as a disturbed breathing pattern rather than as a disease. This updated model of asthma regards it as an adaptation to a stressor. In response to some stress, whether emotional or environmental, the breathing pattern changes. This model points researchers to look in two fruitful directions: how to avoid the stressor, and how to correct the breathing pattern.

This is not to say that medicine plays no role in the treatment of asthma. It certainly does and likely will continue to. When people are in the grip of a full-blown asthma episode, powerful drugs are called for, and they often produce near-miraculous results. However, most health practitioners now give a great deal of attention to retraining the breath of asthmatics. By learning to breathe correctly and by handling the emotions that often trigger asthma, many if not most asthmatics can enjoy a greatly enhanced degree of well-being.

Nutritional and Psychological Observations

Most asthmatics have had considerable exposure to useful information about certain aspects of their problem. For example, my asthma patients are often highly vigilant about allergens and environmental pollutants. They tend to be less well informed about two areas—nutrition and breath retraining—that are crucial in their treatment. I can think of two reasons that these areas are neglected. First, in regard to nutrition, the facts are not all in on what foods cause problems for asthmatics. Any food can be an allergen if the person is in an aroused emotional state. Second, breath retraining is often downplayed because it is hard work for both client and therapist. A great deal of patience is required in the process, and asthma patients—particularly younger ones—are notoriously quick to grow frustrated. And when they get upset, they often have asthma attacks, which are difficult to "ride out" without resorting to medical interventions to stop the attack. In my work with asthma patients, however, I devote most of my time to helping them learn healthy breathing patterns, and some time exploring nutritional issues.

Many asthmatics find that some foods trigger their breathing difficulties. Sometimes this is due to specific toxins occurring in those foods. The list of potentially troublesome foods is quite long, but among the most common are: milk and dairy products, red meat, chocolate, refined sugar, wheat flour, and monosodium glutamate. If you are asthmatic, you would be wise to monitor your consumption of these foods, noticing carefully your body's response after eating them.

In other cases, a psychological connection triggers the problem. For example, one client became symptomatic after eating ice cream but not other dairy products. When we explored some of his childhood patterns, he recalled the following episode, which occurred repeatedly. His mother would get upset with him, spank him, and send him to his room. He would begin to wheeze and exhibit asthma symptoms. His mother would get scared and comfort him, often with ice cream. You can see how ice cream got locked into the association with his mixed feelings toward his mother and the breathing problem. Later in life, he would occasionally get asthma symptoms after having an ice-cream cone with his wife.

It is always useful for the asthmatic to study carefully what emotions came up just before the symptoms started. Two emotions in particular are often "in the air." These are anger and sadness. Something happens that triggers anger or sadness. The person hides these feelings, not acknowledging them to himself or to the people around him. Shortly thereafter, sometimes within minutes, asthma symptoms appear. This also occurs in therapy sessions with asthmatics; symptoms often appear as they talk about difficult emotional situations, particularly in childhood.

It is also very important for asthmatics to study carefully what the "pay-off" is and was in childhood for their asthma episodes. Very often they find one or more of three pay-offs: being comforted or nurtured in an unusually intense or prolonged manner, getting an opportunity to rest and be separate from other family members, and having an excuse to avoid an undesired activity. By noticing these pay-offs, the asthmatic can find other, less painful ways of getting the same needs met.

Now let's turn to the activities themselves. Anyone with respiratory difficulties can benefit from the lessons given earlier in the book, although of course they should consult with their doctor before starting this (or any other) program. In addition to the Foundation and Advanced Lessons, I ask my asthmatic clients to do several other activities each day that are specifically tailored to this problem. Most often, I begin with the following activities, then teach the Foundation and Advanced Lessons later.

If you are asthmatic, have a friend or helper with you while you are doing the following activities. A support person can read them to you and help you master them. Have a glass of water at hand, and drink frequently as you practice. Keeping moist is important, especially in climates like the one I live in, where the air is very dry. But even if you live in a humid climate, extra breathing can dry out the sensitive passages of your airways. Be doubly vigilant of staying in the comfort zone. As you improve the oxygenation of your body, you may feel dizzy from time to time. Pause if you feel this or any other unusual sensation. Rest until it has passed, or return to the activities on another occasion. Better to take them slow and easy.

RESPIRATORY ACTIVITY ONE

Breathing into Your Abdomen

INSTRUCTIONS

Sit upright in a straight-backed chair. Place your hands on your sides, at the bottom of your ribs. Your fingers are pointed toward your navel, and your thumbs toward the back.

Notice that this position of your hands gives you feedback on the movement of your abdomen to the front, side, and back. Breathe in and out of your nose very slowly. Breathe into your abdomen, so that you can feel it swell to the front, side, and back with each in-breath. Keep the breath out of your chest. Focus on getting it "down and in" on the in-breath. On the out-breath, feel your abdomen narrow in the front, side, and back.

Keep breathing very slowly and deeply. Pay particular attention to the swelling of your abdomen to the sides and back. It is easier to feel it swell toward the front, but make sure you can feel your sides and back swell, too.

Practice slowly for two to three minutes, then rest.

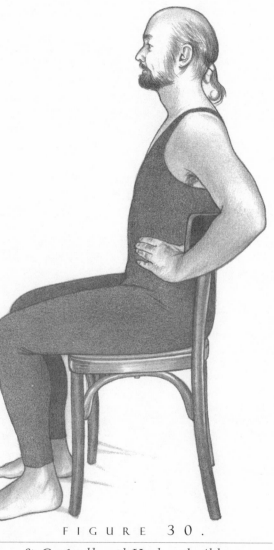

FIGURE 30.

Sit Comfortably, with Hands on the Abdomen

RESPIRATORY ACTIVITY TWO

Taking a Full Out-Breath

This activity, along with the next one, is designed to deal with a problem specific to asthmatics: the tendency not to take a full out-breath. They tend to hold air in, particularly high in their chests. The psychological issue behind this habit, based on my discussions with asthmatics, is that they are reluctant to let go of the air, for fear that they will not get another breath. If you are asthmatic, breath retraining requires that you learn how to let go comfortably of your out-breath, secure in the knowledge that another one is free for the taking.

INSTRUCTIONS

Sit upright in a straight-backed chair. Place one hand on your navel, the other hand on your chest. As you breathe, keep the breath down in your abdomen. Use the hand on your chest to monitor the asthmatic tendency to breathe up in the chest.

Breathe into your abdomen, feeling it swell. Take your in-breath through your nose. As the breath comes in, tilt your chin up, so that the front of your body gets longer. Then when you breathe out, slowly bend forward as if to squeeze all the breath out of your belly. Breathe out through your pursed lips, as if you were blowing out a birthday candle.

The sequence: Breathe into your abdomen, through your nose, lengthening the front of your body. As soon as your belly is full, lean forward slowly, expelling all the air through your pursed lips. Keep bending forward until all the air is expelled. Then sit back up as you breathe in again.

Repeat the sequence slowly for about two minutes.

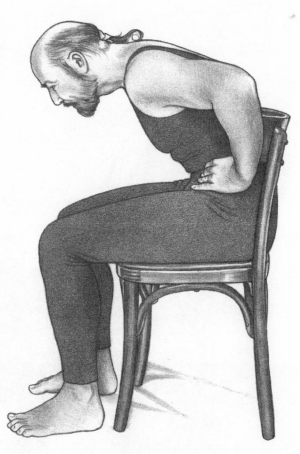

FIGURE 31.

Breathe Deeply on the In-Breath, Then Lean Forward on the Out-Breath

FIGURE 32.

Make the Candle Flicker with the Out-Breath

RESPIRATORY ACTIVITY THREE

Lengthening and Deepening the Out-Breath

This and the next activity were originally designed for use with children, but we later found that adults enjoyed and benefited from them, too. This is the only activity for which you will need a prop. You can use a candle or an old-fashioned clothespin. If you are going to use a candle, light it and place it on a surface a foot or two in front of you. If you are going to use a clothespin, clip a strip of paper two to three inches long into the pin and set it on a surface a foot or two in front of you. The goal during this activity will be to make the flame (or the strip of paper) flicker with your out-breath. Instructions will be given as if a candle is being used.

INSTRUCTIONS

Sit upright, and place your hands at the bottom of your rib cage, fingers toward the navel, thumbs toward your back. Take a deep breath into your abdomen, feeling it swell to the front, back, and side. Purse your lips, as if playing a flute, and blow a steady, strong stream of air toward the flame. Do your best to make the flame bend without blowing it out. Keep moving it farther away from you as you practice. Your goal is to see how far you can get it from you while still making the flame bend with your breath. Focus on taking a complete out-breath, down to the "very last drop" of air. Then take a deep, slow in-breath and repeat the sequence.

As you practice, feel the abdomen swell with the in-breath and narrow with the out-breath. Stay in the comfort zone and never strain. If you get tired or experience any unpleasant sensation, stop and rest.

Practice for two to three minutes, then rest.

RESPIRATORY ACTIVITY FOUR

Coordinating Breathing with Integrated Body Movement

Now we will enter the Olympics of coordinating the mind and body with the breath. This activity integrates the brain hemispheres and links unified brain function with breath and body movement. Children love it because it gives them a genuine challenge and a genuine sense of mastery when they get everything working. Adults take longer and sometimes get frustrated before they break through into mastery.

INSTRUCTIONS

Stand with your feet hip-width apart. Breathe slowly in and out, focusing the breath "down and in" to your abdomen. Take three to four seconds for your in-breath and the same time for your out-breath. Pay attention to the rest of your body, too, so that you do not tense up by trying too hard as this activity proceeds.

Stretch your arms straight out in front of you, as if you were pointing at the horizon. As you slowly breathe, trace a horizontal infinity sign or figure eight with your arms. Follow the direction of movement in Figure 33.

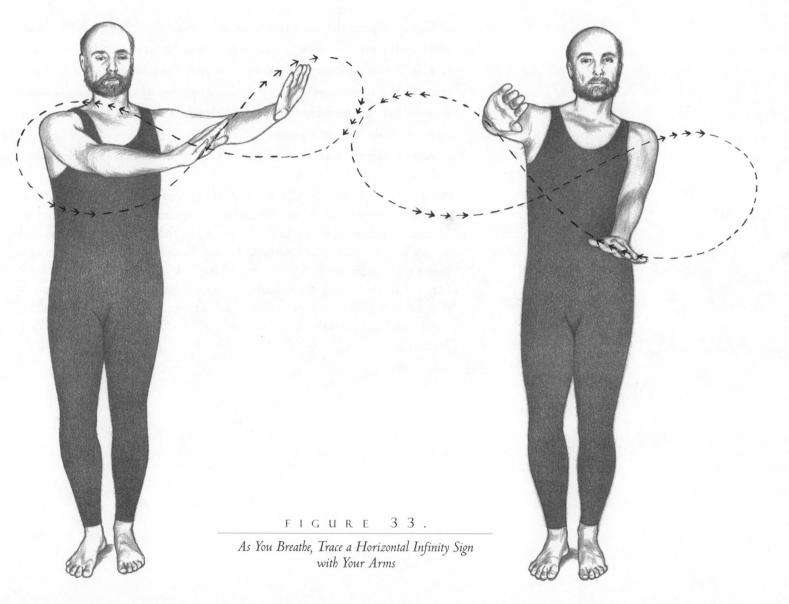

FIGURE 33.

*As You Breathe, Trace a Horizontal Infinity Sign
with Your Arms*

Slowly repeat the movement about twenty-five times. Follow your arms with your eyes. Notice carefully if you hit any "glitches" or hesitancies in the movement, your eyes, or your breathing. If you notice a place in the movement where it feels ragged or where your consciousness wavers, go past that place very slowly and consciously the next time you make the movement.

After you have done the movement twenty-five times, pause and rest.

Asthma can feel like a frightening and complex problem, but the solutions are often quite simple. In my experience, retraining the breath so that one breathes diaphragmatically is the most direct and immediately beneficial treatment. I recommend that the asthmatic think in terms of practicing a lifelong program of conscious breathing. As a rule of thumb, I have found that mastery of these activities takes about a month of daily practice for each year that a person has had asthma. Be patient, and practice slowly and deliberately, keeping your goal in mind: a lifetime of free breathing.

CHAPTER 9

Breathing Together

Breathwork for Couples

ONE OF THE MAIN FOCUSES OF OUR INSTITUTE is our work with committed couples. Our typical format is a three-day intensive, in which the couple comes to Colorado to work with my wife and me for four to six hours a day. They usually stay in a hotel or a bed and breakfast a few blocks away. Our challenge is to help them transform problems that have often been present in their relationship for decades. To help make this happen, we have developed a number of powerful activities that couples can do as homework during the hours when we are not working with them directly.

Although many of the activities involve verbal dialogue, some are purely nonverbal, using breathing, movement, and artwork. Interestingly enough, it is the nonverbal activities that often bring about the most rapid transformations in our clients. I think this is because such breathing activ-

. . . the breathing in unison of lovers
whose bodies smell of each other
Who think the same thoughts without
need of speech
And babble the same speech without
need of meaning . . .
—T. S. ELIOT

ities shift people out of their normal state of consciousness for a while. They may have been trying to solve a relationship problem in their normal state of consciousness for years, only to feel it shift as the result of an altered-state experience provided by one of the activities. I will describe here three of the Couples' Activities we use that involve conscious breathing. The first two are designed to enhance intimacy in general. The third is specifically aimed at increasing sexual pleasure.

COUPLES' ACTIVITY ONE

Tuning In to Each Other's Breathing

INSTRUCTIONS

Lie down side by side, close enough so that you can reach over and touch the abdomen of your partner. If you find you tend to fall asleep, you may do this activity side by side in chairs.

For now, lie comfortably on your back, with your arms down at your sides. Take a moment to get comfortable. When you are settled, direct your attention to your breathing. Just listen to it. Do not try to change it in any way, but simply feel how and where it is moving. Feel the sensations of your breath as it comes and goes from your body. Continue listening to your breathing for a minute or so.

Now reach over and place your hand gently on your partner's abdomen. Notice if your own breathing shifts as a result of being touched. There are no right or wrong answers in this activity; just notice what you experience.

Begin listening to your partner's breathing. Feel the sensations of your hand as it rides up and down. Listen to the rhythm, the speed of the breathing. Tune in to the qualities of the breath. Does it have a quality of ease? Is it labored? Hesitant? Strong? Focus all your attention on receiving the sensations themselves.

Tune in to your partner's breathing for a minute or so.

Now begin consciously to match your partner's breathing. Give yourself plenty of time to make the transition. It's all right if it takes five or ten breaths for you to get linked up. Aim toward matching the rhythm and quality of each other's breathing. You may link up for a few breaths, only to get out of harmony for the next few. That is perfectly natural. Just notice when you get out of synchrony and keep coming back to harmonizing your breathing together.

Continue matching each other's breathing for the next two or three minutes.

When you get to a good stopping place, bring your hand back down to your side again.

FIGURE 34.

Let Your Hand Rest on Your Partner's Abdomen

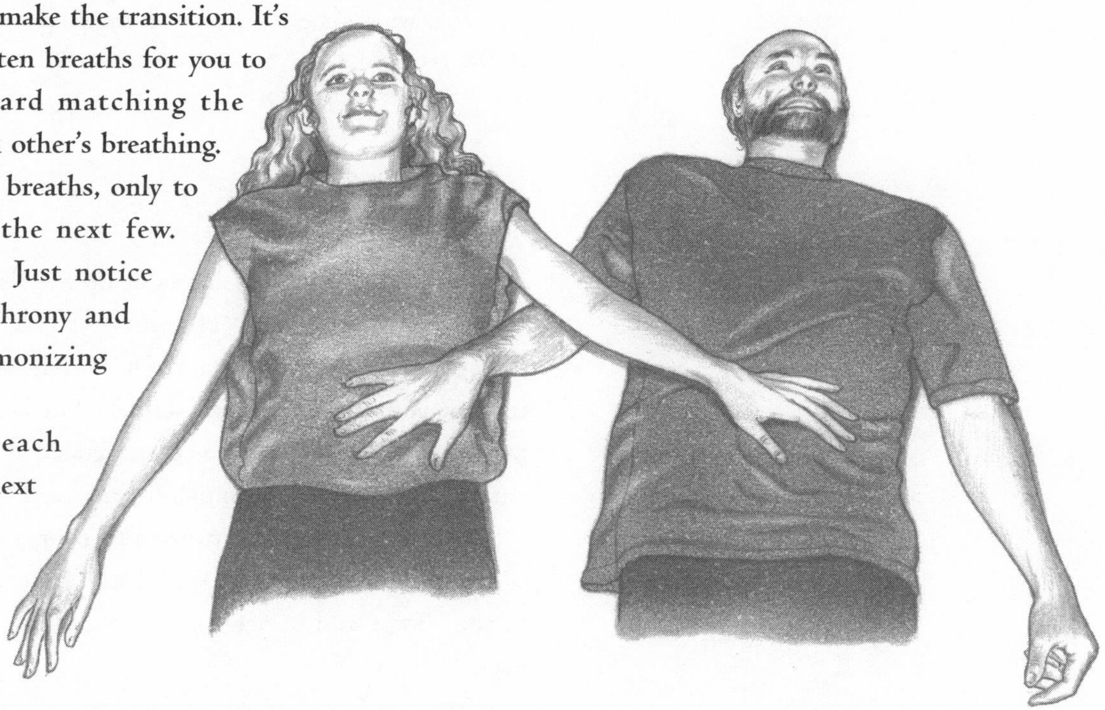

Tune in to your own breathing for a while. Notice its rhythm, its feel. Notice if you feel any differently inside yourself after the period of listening to your partner's breathing.

When you are ready, sit up and talk about what you experience.

COUPLES' ACTIVITY TWO

Breathing with Eye Contact

The following practice is an advanced variation of Activity One. It involves eye contact as well as hand contact, a difference that sounds subtle but is actually quite noticeable.

INSTRUCTIONS

Sit face to face, either in chairs or on the floor.

Join hands and make eye contact. Throughout this process, do your best to maintain eye contact. Of course you will blink from time to time or your attention may wander, but keep coming back to eye contact again. Get your body as comfortable as you can, so that you can sit without moving around much for the next few minutes.

Over the next minute, tune in to your own breath rhythm. Don't try to change your breathing—just listen to it. Notice where you can feel it in your body, and notice the speed and depth with which it comes and goes.

After a minute or so of listening to your own breathing, begin noticing the rise and fall of your partner's breath. At the same time, stay in touch with your own breathing. Your awareness is now directed toward two things: the feeling of your own breathing, and the sight of your partner's breathing, all the while maintaining your primary contact with your partner's eyes. Incorporate all these in your awareness for the next few minutes.

Now close your eyes for two minutes or so. Through sound and touch, tune in to each other's breathing as you stay in tune with your own.

Open your eyes, and resume your eye contact with each other. Begin consciously to match each other's breathing. Give yourself plenty of time to make the transition to being in synchrony. It is also natural for you to drift out of sync, then reconnect. When you notice you have drifted, simply return your breathing to being matched with your partner's.

After two or three minutes, let go of matching your partner's breathing. Tune back in to your own breath for a little while. Then let go of hand and eye contact and rest for a while before discussing what you experienced.

FIGURE 35.

Sit Comfortably, Making Eye Contact

COUPLES' ACTIVITY THREE

Breathing to Enhance Sexual Sensation

We teach the following activity to all couples who wish to enhance their sexual experience. The key aspect of the activity is the subtle tightening and relaxing of the muscles just above the pubic bone. If this is done carefully and slowly, in accordance with the instructions, the practitioner will usually begin to feel a distinct awakening of sexual sensation within a few minutes. With continued practice, many people report an enhanced degree of pleasure during lovemaking. When I teach it to couples in my office, they are fully dressed; many report that it is also enjoyable without clothing as a prelude to lovemaking. You may also do this exercise alone.

INSTRUCTIONS

O my beloved, perhaps in the sky of longing worlds have been born of our love — Just as our breathing, in and out, builds a cradle for life and death?
—NELLY SACHS

Lie down on your side, facing your partner. Many couples enjoy looking into each other's eyes during this activity. Use your intuition in this regard, because other couples like to close their eyes and let their consciousness go deeply inside themselves.

You may rest your head on a cushion or on your upstretched arm. A good place to rest your other arm is on your hip.

Bring up your knees until they are at a comfortable angle, approximately forty-five degrees. Experiment with the angle until you feel that the deep muscles of your lower abdomen are at their most relaxed.

You will be breathing deeply and slowly into your deep belly. As you breathe, you will be tightening and relaxing the muscles between your

navel and the top of your pubic bone. Find this area with your fingers
by pressing the soft place two to three inches beneath your navel;
tighten and relax these muscles a few times to feel the difference
between tension and relaxation in them. If you cannot isolate
these muscles, here is a trick. Purse your lips and blow
hard, as if you were blowing out birthday candles.
Feel the muscles tighten as you blow and relax
when you stop.

Begin the practice as follows. Tighten the
muscles above your pubic bone as you breathe
out slowly. When the in-breath comes in, relax
the muscles completely. Let the out-breath
be long and slow, tightening the muscles all the
way to the end of the out-breath. At the end of
the out-breath, squeeze the muscles gently as if you were
squeezing "the last drop" of breath out. Then let the muscles relax
and "flop open" as you breathe in slowly. Repeat this ten or twelve times,
placing your attention on the sensations of the pelvis.

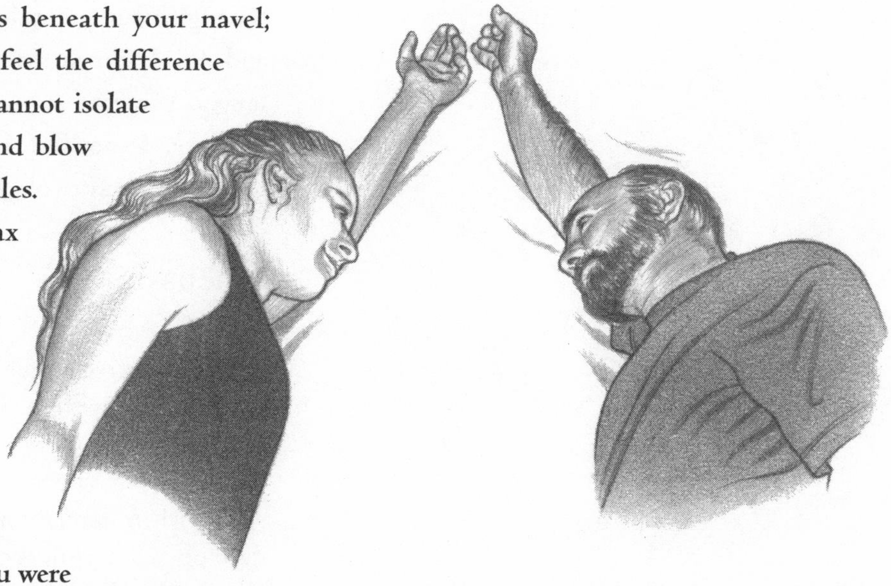

After ten or twelve breaths, let the process become more subtle. Make
the squeezing very slight on the out-breath, almost as if you were
imagining it. Continue to let the muscles "flop open" on the in-breath.
Practice this subtler form of the process for another ten to twelve breaths.

Now let go of the tightening and relaxing, focusing your attention
on breathing very deeply and slowly into the area you have been tensing. Aim your breathing for the area just above your pubic bone, allowing it to move gently with your breathing.

FIGURE 36.

Lie on Your Sides, Facing Each Other

By now you may begin to feel waves of sexual sensation streaming through your genitals. Favor these with the breath, breathing slowly and deeply down through these sensations. Stay with the sensations as long as you can.

If you do not feel the waves of sensation begin to stream within fifteen to twenty minutes of practice, come back to the activity again another day.

DISCUSSION

I taught this technique to a thirty-one-year-old woman who consulted my wife and me with an unusual request. She had engaged mainly in sexual relationships with women since her teenage years. An incest survivor, she had never felt safe with men, nor had she consummated a sexual relationship with a man. Now, entering a different phase of her life, she had developed a strong bond with a man, with whom she desired a sexual relationship. But, she told us, she felt a complete absence of any sensation in her genitals when they embraced and made initial movements toward lovemaking. Was there anything she could do to increase sensation?

Using the previous activity, we worked with her for about half an hour. The first ten minutes were hard because she had a difficult time isolating the muscles involved. Suddenly she "got it," though, and a look of ease spread over her face. After ten more minutes, the look of ease was replaced by a blissful smile. We could tell at a glance that she had discovered sensation in her pelvis. As part of her homework, we asked her to do the activity with her friend. The next week brought a very positive report. The breathing activity had taught her how to surrender to pleasure, she said, rather than tense against it. This had enabled them to enjoy several mutually pleasurable sexual experiences.

CHAPTER 10

Enhancing Sports Performance

Everything I have written in Parts I and II of this book is applicable to athletes who want to enhance their performance. In this chapter I want to give more detailed instructions for three additional techniques that athletes I've worked with have found helpful. These techniques relate to concentration and endurance—two areas in which athletes are always looking for an edge.

Before describing the specific techniques, there are several general comments I want to make about sports and breathing. First, I have been quite amazed at the high number of proficient athletes who suffer from breathing problems. I can think of half a dozen fine athletes who are asthmatic, for example, and many more than that who had other flaws in their breathing when I first worked with them. On the surface you would think that competitive sports is the last place to look for an asthmatic. But we humans are a tenacious and resilient lot, capable of overcoming great adversity if the persistence is there. Many athletes have built an outstanding performance career on top of a very disturbed breathing pattern. Very few people knew that my fellow Coloradan, the great mountain climber Roger Marshall, was asthmatic. Before he was killed in a solo Himalayan ascent, he had scaled K2 and other formidable peaks. A companion of his told me that Roger would sometimes sit in a chair for days before an ascent, willfully getting his asthma under control.

There are probably many reasons a person with breathing difficulties would be drawn to athletics, but here are two that athletes have uncovered in their discussions with me. First, many athletes are, in essence, running away from their feelings. The vigorous physiological stress of sports has a flushing effect on the body, much as a good cry provides. Numerous sports stars have told me that to cry or show a tender emotion is very difficult for them, and that exercise takes their minds off their troublesome issues, problems, and feelings.

The second reason extends into childhood and the genesis of both their psychological issues and their use of athletics as a coping skill. Sometimes an athletic persona is built on top of an emotional problem and its accompanying breathing difficulties. For example, one basketball player I worked with used sports as a way to cope with a painful conflict between his father and mother. His father was an athlete and a coach, and my client's devotion to sports was a covert way of siding with his father. Later in life he found that he was growing disenchanted with sports. When he worked with this issue in therapy, he found that he was really disenchanted with the role sports had played in his life. When he did the early-childhood therapy work, his love for sports returned because it was no longer contaminated by his unresolved issues about his mother and father.

From this perspective, it can be seen that all of the concepts and practices of conscious breathing we have covered in this book would be directly applicable to sports.

A second general comment is that these techniques are as useful to the beginner or amateur as they are to the professional. When I was first studying breathing in the early 1970s, I ran an experiment with a group of sixth-grade girls who were playing basketball in gym class. We let one group shoot foul shots while a second group sat with their eyes closed. Instead of actually shooting baskets, this second group repeated the following mind-body sequence: Take a deep breath, and visualize a successful foul shot. After twenty minutes, we had each girl in the class go to the foul line and shoot ten shots in a row. The breath/visualization group greatly outperformed the group that had been actually shooting baskets. The girls on the court were amazed, as was their physical education teacher, but it was the experimenters who were really thrilled. This little experiment let me know that mind/body skills like conscious breathing and mental imagery could be of benefit to people with minimal athletic skill.

And thank goodness, because although I am enthusiastic, I am definitely in the unnatural rather than natural athlete category. As my golf teacher said upon observing me for the first time, "I don't know if there's such a thing as a natural golf swing, but if there is, you definitely haven't got it." So please do not think you need to be a world-class athlete to benefit from conscious breathing. I have used all three of these techniques extensively in my own active sports life, with uniformly excellent results. With that in mind, let me share with you the three specialized techniques I have taught to amateurs and professionals alike.

ATHLETES' TECHNIQUE ONE

Increasing Stamina

I have personally used this technique in running, walking, and bicycling. My students have used it in these and a number of other sports, including swimming and cross-country skiing.

I had ample opportunity to test it not long after I began to use it in the mid-eighties. The hardest work I have ever asked of my body was hiking and biking in the Himalayas of Nepal and Tibet. In Tibet especially I was reduced to tears on several occasions because of the difficulty of the terrain and its demands on my body. Often I was riding all day at 14,000 feet and going over passes that were several thousand feet higher. This conscious breathing technique was of immense help in getting me through many arduous situations.

The basic technique involves lengthening the breath through a specific type of breath-counting, meanwhile coordinating it with the rhythm of your arms or legs. Since I mainly use it biking and hiking, my experience is in coordinating my breath with leg movement.

INSTRUCTIONS

To keep it simple, let's learn it in relation to walking. Imagine walking along at a moderate pace. Select an odd number to use at first, usually 3, 5, or 7. Time your in-breath to this count and your out-breath to the same count. If you are using 5, for example, you would count: In-2-3-4-5, Out-2-3-4-5. Time each step to go with each count, five steps to the in-breath, five steps to the out-breath. If you started the count on your left foot, you would take five steps on your in-breath—left, right, left, right, left—then switch to your out-breath, beginning with your right foot.

Always use an odd number, so that you will start each count on a different foot. If you use an even number you will feel a subtle favoring of the foot that begins the counts, with a resulting imbalance.

As you experiment, you will find a good number to start with. After a few minutes, begin to lengthen your breath with a longer count. If you have been using 5, shift up to a 7-count. When you are comfortable in that zone, try a 9-count.

If you are really exerting yourself, you may have to shift down to a shorter, faster breath like a 3-count. As you become more comfortable with your pace, start lengthening your breath again. Always stay in the zone of comfort, though. If you find yourself straining, change numbers until you find the pace that feels good.

DISCUSSION

For endurance sports, such as running or cycling, staying "within your breath" is a central idea. If you stay inside your breath, you tend not to tire easily, and you have energy left over for an occasional "kick" or sprint. If you exert yourself "outside your breath," you build up an oxygen debt in your body that has to be cashed in eventually. The technique I have just described is an ideal way to stay inside your breath. By counting and lengthening your breath, you make use of your own natural powers of mind to coach yourself as you go. I predict you will be amazed at the immediate results you get. Nearly everyone I know who has learned this technique has reported a noticeable effect on their endurance from the beginning.

ATHLETES' TECHNIQUE TWO

Honing Concentration

I alluded to this technique in Chapter 2, and now I would like to give more precise directions on how to apply it to any sport where relaxed concentration is required. I have personally used it with golf swings, tennis serves, and basketball foul shots. Students have applied it to other sports with which I am not familiar, such as wrestling and target shooting. It relies upon two simple but powerful truths about how the human body operates.

The first truth: It is not possible to feel anxious while breathing abdominally. The quickest way to clear anxiety out of your body is to take a few deep belly-breaths. Chest-breathing is wired into the anxiety-producing mechanisms of the body, while belly-breathing is wired into the relaxation-producing mechanisms. If you are anxious, you can wait until you are not anxious and your breathing will slow down. But if you are in a hurry to clear out the anxiety, you can slow your breath down consciously. Sure enough, the anxiety will go away.

The second truth relates to truth itself. If you tell the truth, your body relaxes slightly. This principle underlies the mechanism known as the lie detector. The lie detector measures very tiny changes in anxiety reactions like sweat production. When you are anxious, your palms sweat slightly (and, as some of us know, quite profusely if we are very anxious). The lie detector simply measures these variables and prints them out on a page. When you tell the truth, there is an immediate shift toward decreased sweat production. In the following technique, we make use of these two anxiety-canceling phenomena: breath and truth.

Let me use as an example a transcript from my teaching of the technique to a fine golfer. Robert had been playing golf since he was a child, but at midlife he was still seeking improvement. Golf is an ideal place to apply the technique, because, while some sports are games of inches, golf is a game of millimeters. A microscopic movement of your head can mean the difference between a beautiful shot and an embarrassing gaffe. In golf, as in many other sports, focus is everything.

GAY: Take a couple of practice swings, then address the ball, Robert. *(He takes a few practice swings with his seven-iron, then squares to face the ball.)*

As you stand ready to hit the ball, take a big belly-breath, and after the out-breath, say something true. Anything will do. One reliable truth is to report a body sensation. Say something like "My neck is tight," or "I'm feeling hungry." The only requirement is that it be unarguable. Another possibility is to say something true about your relationship to the world. "I'm looking at the ball" is an example, as is "I'm standing on the grass." It doesn't have to be profound, just as long as it's true.

ROBERT *(takes a deep breath):* I'm feeling good right now. *(He hits the ball squarely, and I lean over and place another ball on the ground for him to hit.)*

GAY: Let's do it again before you have a chance to think about it much. Take a nice, big relaxed breath in and out, then say something true just before your swing.

ROBERT *(takes a breath and exhales):* I'm feeling my belt against my stomach. *(He hits another shot, this time drawing it a little to the left. It's still a solid shot, though.)*

GAY *(placing another ball):* One more time. Take a big, relaxed breath and say something unarguable just before you swing.

ROBERT *(takes his breath):* It's Wednesday. *(He swings and connects again, hitting a nice 130-yarder just short of the pin.)*

GAY: I think you've got the hang of it. Keep it very simple. Just take a relaxed, full breath, then say something true. If you feel uncomfortable saying the truth out loud, just subvocalize it to yourself.

DISCUSSION

That's all there is to it. Take a deep breath, and tell the truth. This puts the body and mind into alignment, freeing the attention to focus on the outcome. Come to think of it, perhaps this would be a good technique to apply not only to sports but to life in general.

ATHLETES' TECHNIQUE THREE
Quickly Coming into the Present

One of the big problems all athletes face is how to get focused on the here and now. If you watch sports on television, pay attention sometime to how the best athletes get back into the present after making a bad shot or committing a foul. The most successful have some kind of reliable technique for shaking off a negative experience and "getting back into the game." As in much of life, success in sports has as much to do with how you let go of the past as it does with how good you are in the present.

The finest athletes have worked long and hard to be able to snap back after a disappointing shot or time at bat. Others are unable to shake the past, and it becomes a weight on them that is actually visible from the stands.

The purpose of this technique is to release the past and get into the present. Although I describe it here as a sports technique, it works superbly well in the rest of the game of life.

INSTRUCTIONS

The technique is to catch yourself as soon as possible after a negative experience, take three deep breaths, and change your body position. Let's say you have just struck out with the bases loaded. You feel disgusted with yourself, so you take off your helmet and bang it on the ground. At this point, you hear boos and grow even more disgusted with yourself. You catch yourself "going negative," starting to lock a bad feeling in your body and a bad attitude in your mind. Remembering your technique, you take three big, deep breaths and change your body position. At the end of the third big breath you give yourself a shake and relax your shoulders. You feel good again. The past is past. You are ready for the next time.

DISCUSSION

This technique is based on a solid understanding of how the body operates. Experiment with yourself, and you may come to the same conclusion

I have reached: It is hard to maintain a bad mood for long if you breathe deeply and shift your body position. Part of the mechanism of a bad mood is shallow breathing and frozen body postures. Practically speaking, I have experimented in my therapy practice for years to find the minimum number of breaths required to shift a negative mood. Three is the magic number, if you also include a conscious change of body position. If you are not moving your body, approximately twenty deep breaths will usually shift a mood. Sixty breaths are the most I have seen it take before a bad mood began to lighten up.

Frequently Asked Questions About Breathing

IN THIS CHAPTER I WILL PASS ALONG BRIEF ANSWERS to some of the questions most frequently asked in trainings, lectures, and classes. Some of the answers cover material that is elaborated upon in previous chapters.

QUESTION: Is there one major breathing problem that you see more than anything else?

ANSWER: Yes. It is the tendency to restrict the breathing by holding the belly muscles too tight. This excess tension forces the breath up into the chest and keeps the diaphragm from going through its full range of motion. The solution is simple, but it can take a great deal of practice to master: Soften the belly muscles, and breathe so that the abdomen expands with the in-breath.

QUESTION: When you say to "breathe into the belly," what do you mean? There's no air going into the stomach, is there?

ANSWER: No air goes into the stomach. Breathing into the belly means that you take a full enough breath that the diaphragm can flatten downward. This pushes the contents of the abdominal cavity downward and outward. If your belly muscles are relaxed, you will get a rounding of the belly on the in-breath.

QUESTION: I can get a breath into my belly, but my chest feels contracted and tight. When should I breathe up in my chest?

ANSWER: Paradoxically, the deeper you can breathe into your belly, the higher you can breathe into your chest. Ideally, if you get a full breath so that your belly expands, your chest will open up to the perfect degree. Do not force breath up into your chest. Go down and in with the breath, letting your chest expand at the end of the belly-breath. In healthy breathing, the chest does not move a great deal—just a little at the end of the downward and outward expansion of the abdomen.

QUESTION: There are books that say to breathe in through the nose and out through the mouth. What do you recommend?

ANSWER: Breathe through the nose both in and out. Some techniques may have you breathe through the mouth for a special reason, but for most normal situations breathing should be done through the nose.

QUESTION: Is there a need to tighten muscles on the in-breath or the out-breath?

ANSWER: When you are learning to breathe correctly, you can tighten your belly muscles on the out-breath. This will help you learn to take a complete out-breath, by encouraging you to squeeze the breath out "'till the very last drop.'" Doing this will also help you learn to relax your belly muscles on the in-breath. But later, once you have learned how to breathe correctly, you will not need to tighten any muscles during either inspiration or exhalation.

QUESTION: Doing the Foundation Lessons, I sometimes feel the same sensations I feel just before an orgasm. Is this normal?

ANSWER: Completely normal. Once you learn to breathe effectively, every breath will trigger pleasant streaming sensations. I once asked a roomful of my advanced breathwork students how many had noticed an improvement in their sexual experience since practicing the breathing program. Nearly all of them raised their hands. The breathing lessons enhance the body's ability to feel positive energy in general, so it stands to reason that sexual feelings would be triggered by them.

QUESTION: When I have breathed deeply for a while, I sometimes smell and taste something gassy. It has a slightly metallic taste and a smell like nail polish remover. What is this?

ANSWER: I lean toward two explanations. The simpler possibility is that you are smelling and tasting gases that are by-products of digestion or lack thereof. For example, if you have not eaten for a while before your breathing session, your body may be producing ketones. These substances have a sweetish smell. An emergency room doctor I know told me that around the ER this condition is known colloquially as "fruity-breath."

The other possibility is that anesthesia from old surgeries or birth itself is being discharged through the deeper breathing. It is hard to conceive of how it could stay in the body for that long a time, but I have had enough experiences of this sort to keep me open to the possibility. Some diseases can stay in the body for generations, so it does not seem outside the realm of possibility that a gas could bond cellularly for a long time, only to be released later through deep breathing.

QUESTION: How does the breathwork you teach compare with the type I learned in natural childbirth classes?

ANSWER: Our form of breathwork resembles more the Bradley Method than the Lamaze Method. The latter uses a shorter panting breath, while Bradley teaches a slower, deeper breath. In childbirth, any breathing is better than no breathing at all! I have coached at births with the techniques in this book with excellent results, but I have also talked with hundreds of women who got good results with Bradley and Lamaze. I think breathing to manage the pain of childbirth is a wonderful use of this technology.

QUESTION: I have trouble lying down for any length of time because of back trouble. Can these activities be done sitting up?

ANSWER: Yes, they can. You may need to modify the instructions slightly, but I have had clients who learned all of them sitting up, with excellent results.

QUESTION: What happens during hyperventilation? How can I prevent it?

ANSWER: If you do the activities in the book as instructed, you won't ever hyperventilate. Hyperventilation involves breathing in an imbalanced way so that too much carbon dioxide is discharged. This throws off the acid/alkaline balance of the blood. In its extreme form, hyperventilation leads to tetany: The fingers become cramped in a splayed configuration, the head feels constricted, and the mouth draws into an O. Although essentially harmless, it can scare the daylights out of the person experiencing it. Milder symptoms of hyperventilation include frequent sighing, short breaths that are largely in the chest, dizziness, and mild anxiety.

If you started to hyperventilate in a doctor's office, he or she would probably have you breathe into a paper bag, saturating your blood with carbon dioxide and restoring the balance. If you started to hyperventilate

in my office, I would invite you to contact the emotion you were concealing and breathe into it. After a few deep belly-breaths into the fear, anger,
or sadness, you would probably have a release of the emotion and feel
better than you did before. I say this with some confidence because I have
witnessed this same sequence hundreds of times. There is usually an emotional trigger that starts the hyperventilation. If you can identify and deal
with the emotion, the hyperventilation fades quickly.

QUESTION: I drift off to sleep or space out when I'm doing the
breathing lessons. Should I try to keep myself awake or let myself drift
off?

ANSWER: My recommendation is to let yourself drift off, then pick
up the lesson again when you come back. Sometimes going to sleep simply means that you're tired and need some extra rest. Some people, however, use sleep as a mechanism of avoidance. I have had clients who had a
pattern of going to sleep during breathwork sessions when specific emotions would surface. You might want to tune in to when you get sleepy
and what feelings and thoughts you have just prior to the sleepiness. This
might give you insight into whether your sleepiness is driven by the bio-
logical needs of your body or by psychological factors.

After a few practice sessions, you may notice that you can stay alert
throughout the session. In the meantime, though, just enjoy the drifting
off, and resume your breathing when you drift back in.

QUESTION: I find myself pausing at the top of my breath and sometimes at the bottom. What should I do about this?

ANSWER: Ideally, the in-breath should melt into the out-breath, and
vice versa. If you watch a healthy baby breathe, you see a smooth transition between the in-breath and the out-breath. Babies don't stop at the

top or the bottom. In 1951, in one of the first major studies of breathing, a doctor named Clausen noted that the neurotic individuals he was studying tended to have a sharp transition between their inhale and exhale. Something about the traumas of life seems to interfere with our ability to make a smooth transition between in-breath and out-breath. If you notice this tendency, slow down your breathing as much as you can and focus on making a smooth transition. It is never too late to learn. My oldest client to date with this breathing pattern was seventy-seven when I first worked with her; she is ninety at this writing and still doing her breathing every day.

QUESTION: What do you think of visualizations during breathing?

ANSWER: If you enjoy them and find them useful, great! Some of my clients find them useful; others are indifferent to them. I sometimes use ocean wave imagery to enhance people's ability to get a flowing rhythm to their breathing. This is not an area I work with very much, so I cannot be of much technical help to you beyond recommending that you experiment on your own.

QUESTION: I like to make sounds on the out-breath while I'm practicing the lessons. Is this okay?

ANSWER: Yes. A lot of people like to hum or make "aaah" sounds as they breathe. Even if you are breathing through your nose, you can make all sorts of sounds on your out-breath. A sigh or hum feels good throughout your whole body.

QUESTION: What should I do if some feelings come up while I am breathing?

ANSWER: It is perfectly normal for deeper breathing to bring emotions to the surface. The best thing you can do is slow your breathing down and appreciate the emotional release. Participate with the tears, for example, or focus your attention on the sensations of the anxiety. Keep your breath going, slow and relaxed, and avoid judging yourself or the feelings themselves. Feelings are like thunderstorms: they have a beginning, middle, and end. Breathe through the whole evolution of the feeling, from emergence to resolution, and you will come out the other side feeling very refreshed.

QUESTION: Sometimes I get dizzy when I am practicing the lessons. What should I do if this happens?

ANSWER: Dizziness is usually caused by trying too hard. When you first feel the symptoms of light-headedness, relax and breathe even more slowly. If the symptoms continue, pause and rest until it passes. This goes for any unpleasant sensation, such as neck tension or an ache in the ribs. Don't push through symptoms, ease through them or rest through them. All the activities are to be done in the comfort zone.

Personal History

How I First Became Interested in Conscious Breathing

I CAN TRACE MY INTEREST IN CONSCIOUS BREATHING to a specific moment in the late sixties.

In 1969 I was twenty-four years old and in deep trouble. I weighed close to three hundred pounds, a hundred pounds more than I weigh today. I was burning through two packs of Marlboros a day, and I was stuck in a very bad marriage. About the only thing that was working well in my life was my relationship with my infant daughter, whom I adored and whom I credit with giving me a reason to live through those dark times. I also valued and enjoyed my friendship with Neil Marinello, a fellow teacher and counselor at the small boarding school in New Hampshire where I was employed. One day Neil invited me on an excursion that changed the course of my life.

Neil told me that one of his former professors at Harvard had gone to

India and had a profound spiritual awakening there. He had changed his name to Ram Dass and come back to offer his teachings to America. He was staying at his father's estate a short drive down the road. Would I be interested in meeting him? I had vaguely heard of Ram Dass under his old name of Richard Alpert, when he had come to fame as one of the band of LSD adventurers associated with Timothy Leary. I didn't have anything else to do that Sunday afternoon, so I agreed to go.

Other than having smoked marijuana in college, I was a virtual stranger to the counterculture. I had somehow managed to go through the sixties without ever growing long hair or marching in a demonstration. My passions were on the printed page: I was a literature zealot. My heroes were Proust, Faulkner, John Barth, Donald Barthelme. My aspirations were clear to me. I would put in a few years as a teacher until I could pen the proverbial Great American Novel. Then I would get a divorce and raise my daughter in a cottage on a windswept stretch of Maine coast. I would write, puff thoughtfully on my pipe, pontificate. Boy, was I in for a surprise.

When Neil and I sauntered onto the grounds of the Alpert estate, we were greeted by a dreamy wisp of a girl in a flowing Indian garment. She chirped a blissful welcome and offered us fruit from a basket. She led us to a circle where Ram Dass was sitting with a few of his disciples. My first thought was: What are these people selling? Everybody was dressed in robes and filmy saris; incense lingered in the air. It was a most un–New Hampshire–like scene: I had certainly never witnessed anything like it.

Neil and I spent the afternoon listening to him talk. He spun stories of his Hindu guru, Neem Karoli Baba, and talked of his many spiritual experiences in India. At first I was put off. Ram Dass was entertaining but saccharine and overly mysterious. Taking a break from the mystical to go to the bathroom, I found myself getting more enjoyment out of talking to Ram Dass's father, a dynamic little man who had a tolerant, amused attitude toward the spiritual goings-on taking place on his lawn. He was alert, clear, and full of go-get-'em energy, in sharp contrast to the goofy crew gathered around Ram Dass. He referred to his son as Bubba Rum Dum, but with the tolerant affection that parents somehow manage in the face of their children's weirdness.

As the afternoon went on, however, Ram Dass began to grow on me. After I got past his robe and beads, I began to hear what he was saying. Here was a guy who had the chutzpah to talk about his life, his inner experiences, and his attempts to transform himself. Ram Dass spoke openly of his sexuality—even his homosexuality—and his various emotional difficulties. He talked about his quest to find his inner spiritual connection to God and the universe. Many of his stories centered on his own woodenheadedness in the face of his guru's attempt to enlighten him.

Looking back on it, I don't think it was really the beads and Hindu paraphernalia that caused my initial negative reaction. I think it was the fact that there were so many things I had not faced in my own life. To be around someone so openly expressive was threatening to my stash of unexamined and delicately balanced neuroses. Unconsciously, my skepticism was rooted in a fear: If I once started opening up to the truths I was concealing from myself—my feelings, needs, hurts—I believed I would come apart at the seams.

I cannot remember much of what he talked about that afternoon, but one comment Ram Dass made pointed me in a fruitful new direction. He was touting the practical value of Hindu psychology as opposed to the more cognitive Western version. He said that he had spent ten years in psychoanalysis trying to deal with his anxiety, but at the end he was just as anxious as he'd been before. In other words, after ten years of therapy he *understood* his anxiety, but he still had it. He went on to say that a simple breathing exercise he had learned in India actually decreased his anxiety. But he wouldn't say what the technique was, implying that one would have to go to India to learn it.

For some reason that comment stuck in my mind after Neil and I went home. I was totally uninterested in some aspects of Ram Dass's trip, like worshiping a guru, but the actual practices he had mentioned—yoga, breathing exercises, chanting—fascinated me. I wanted to learn more about them, but I wasn't sure how to proceed. Ram Dass's suggestion—go to India and hang out for a year or two—was easy for him to say. He had no kids and a rich daddy. For me, a pilgrimage to Boston, an hour away, was nearly beyond reach. However, synchronicity soon struck.

In a supermarket the following week I spotted a paperback called *Yoga, Youth and Reincarnation* by Jess Stearn. The title put me off a little (I didn't believe in reincarnation then and still don't), but otherwise it turned out to be very well-written. I was excited by the careful descriptions of the yoga postures, meditation practices, and breathing practices. It seemed to be just what I was looking for, giving all the details that Ram Dass had hinted at but not revealed. So I took it home and put it to work. Midnight found me doing yoga stretches and hunkering down cross-legged for my first attempts at meditation. Three practices I tried that first night made a deep impression on me: alternate-nostril breathing, clench-release relaxation training, and mantra meditation.

The alternate-nostril breathing cleared my mind immediately, even with only a couple of minutes of practice. This was important to me, because one of my biggest problems at the time was getting my mind to stop racing. I was amazed at how quickly and simply the breathing exercise accomplished what my will had failed utterly to do. I also discovered that I had been holding my breath most of my life, which was related to holding my stomach muscles chronically tightened. I mark that evening as the first time in my life I used conscious breathing.

The clench-release relaxation training involved tightening and releasing each muscle group, starting with the fists and working through the whole body. It sounds simple and it is, but in fact it is a very powerful technique for changing consciousness. After twenty minutes of the practice, I felt like I had a brand-new body. I made a discovery that astounded me: I had been tense my whole life and not known it! I hadn't known it because I had no state of relaxation to compare it to. By contrasting tension and re-laxation a few dozen times in the exercise, I had increased my awareness immensely. Most important, the feeling of well-being in my body let me know I was on the right track.

The mantra meditation practice I learned from the book involved clos-ing my eyes and silently repeating the Sanskrit syllable *om* over and over. It worked so well and so quickly that I became an instant true believer in meditation. I think my mind was so starved for transcendence that it took only about two minutes of repeating the mantra before I had a profound mystical experience. At one moment I was repeating the mantra; in the next, my thought processes went completely silent. Where my thoughts had been just a moment before, an all-encompassing white light filled my field of inner awareness. It was as though I had been caught up in the drama of a movie, when suddenly the projector stopped and the white light of the screen became the foreground of my mind. I realized that all my life I had believed I *was* my thoughts! Now I saw that I was a vast ocean of pure consciousness, with thoughts floating by on the surface. I had been so lost in my thoughts all my life that I had missed out on the *being* of being human.

It was a moment that shook up my whole world. Later, I took for-mal instruction in meditation in a Zen monastery and through the

Transcendental Meditation organization, but it was that first two minutes that really got me started. As I write this book my meditation streak continues: I meditate an hour a day and have not missed a day since 1973.

A PIVOTAL EXPERIENCE

At about this same time I got an even stronger lesson, a literal smack on the head that woke me up. I was walking down a country road one day in winter when I slipped on a patch of ice. My feet shot out from under me, and I fell on the back of my head, knocking myself out. (I can personally testify that you actually do see stars, just like in the cartoons.) I was probably out cold for only a couple of minutes, but the experience changed my life's direction. As I hovered in semiconsciousness, I had the ability to see down through the layers of myself to the pure consciousness at the source. I could see my emotional layer, my body layer, and my mind. I could see how each layer obscured the clear-light state of pure consciousness that everything rested in.

Furthermore, I realized that all those layers were shaped by the family script I had bought into without question. I was, in essence, replaying my father's life. He had smoked heavily, had been obese, and had died before he could fulfill his potential. I was on the same path, a path I had never consciously chosen.

There was a profound shift in my breathing while I was unconscious. I was dimly aware that my breathing was deep, full, and free. My breath came in and out with a rush; there were no hesitancies, no glitches, no holding. It felt like a spring wind blowing through me, refreshing every cell. Sadly, though, as I came back into my normal state of consciousness, I "lost my breath." The old strictures came back, and I could feel myself tensing up as my personality reassembled itself. It was as if the stress of not being my true self caused my body to be tense and my breathing to be rough and controlled. But for a few minutes there I had breathed freely! I found myself wondering: Is it possible to breathe that way all the time? Is there a free style of breathing down there inside me waiting to happen? Could I feel that cellular refreshment with each breath all the time? Now I know the answers to those questions—yes, yes, and yes. It just takes daily practice, a much gentler and more effective path than smashing your head on the road.

I got up off the ice a changed man. I decided to figure out what *I* wanted to do with my life. I realized I had not been asking two fundamental questions—Who am I? and What do I want?—and in the absence of that quest I was killing myself.

I dedicated myself to finding the answers. Within the next year I lost a hundred pounds, left my marriage, and moved to the West Coast to pursue my new-found dream of a doctorate in counseling psychology. During this time my breathing became paramount in my awareness. I used it constantly to recenter myself. Remembering that moment of freedom on the ice, when my breath seemed to nurture my very soul, I now had a benchmark to guide me.

I found out from Neil that the University of New Hampshire, just twenty minutes away, had one of the most innovative counseling programs in the country. I signed up and virtually whizzed through the master's degree program, soaking it up like the proverbial sponge. It was there that I found myself and my life's purpose. I had always thought I would go through life bored. Since I began the study of counseling psychology, I have never had even a momentary experience of boredom. That, to me, seems miraculous.

A LIFE-CHANGING SUGGESTION

While I was at UNH I met a key figure in my life, Dwight Webb. A heartful and generous teacher, Dwight has inspired a generation of counseling psychologists over the twenty-five years he has been at UNH. I was speaking to him one day about a conflict I was feeling between counseling and writing. I felt I had to choose one or the other. Dwight asked, Why not do them both? Why not use your passion for writing to write about counseling? Why not write about what you love? It sounds so simple and obvious now, but I had never considered this possibility. I soon began to write poems about the counseling process, and these found their way into print in some of the counseling journals. They caught the eye of two innovative professors at Stanford, John Krumboltz and Carl Thoresen, who invited me to come to California to work toward my doctorate.

In the spring of 1971, my marriage ending, I packed all my earthly belongings into my VW bug. I didn't have much stuff to start with, due to my state of general poverty; the divorce courts had also been helpful in lessening my attachment to material things. I drove to California, where I would soon start the doctoral program at Stanford. My daughter followed a month later, and we took up residence on the campus in a tiny apartment.

Palo Alto in the seventies was a hotbed of psychospiritual ferment. A bookstore there named The Plowshare was a hub for spiritual seekers. The back room was called The Seed Center; it carried only books on esoteric philosophy and Eastern religions. Today there are similar stores in all major cities, but at the time I had never seen anything like it. I was amazed to find literally thousands of books on subjects that I had not known existed. It was here that I got my deeper education. By day, I learned the canon of Western psychology in the hard-nosed, research-oriented style that Stanford favored; by night, I immersed myself in the spiritual traditions. Both streams of wisdom were of equal importance to me, and still are. Western psychology is a powerful tool but lacks heart and soul; Eastern psychology has a solid spiritual grounding but lacks intellectual rigor. Why not have a happy marriage of both? That was what I was looking for.

The Seed Center had dozens of books on breathing. It seemed that every spiritual tradition had something to say about breathing as a path of enlightenment. There were books printed in India—on paper lightly scented with patchouli—that described four-thousand-year-old breathing practices. There were books printed in Hong Kong with titles like *The Taoist Secret of the Primordial Breath*. Frequently the whole book would boil down to a single breathing practice, with an entire philosophy wrapped around it. Sometimes, maddeningly, a book would spend two hundred pages promoting the spiritual value of a particular style of breathing, only to say at the end that it could not be taught in a book. I read them all and remember very little about any of them today, except that they all pointed me toward personal experimentation. If a breathing exercise was described in a book, I would sit down on one of the cushions provided by The Plowshare and try it out on the spot. The Plowshare was the kind of place where no one would ever disturb a browser, so I was able to spend hours in there on my quest. In Appendix B you will find a listing of some of the books on breathing that I have personally found of value.

It was in The Seed Center that I discovered Wilhelm Reich's work on breathing. I have written about my adventures in Reichian therapy in *At the Speed of Life*, so I won't repeat them here. I became fascinated with Reich and read everything I could find, although I would not have enough money to do Reichian therapy or its offshoot, bioenergetics, until several years later. I built some "orgone devices" and performed various Reichian experiments until I grew convinced that Reich's natural science enthusi-asms—in contrast to his work on breathing—were tantalizing but of lit-tle practical use.

Reich's breathwork emphasized deep, rapid breathing through the open mouth. After a while, if this is done with care and/or with skillful help, it will result in an emotional catharsis or deeply pleasurable streaming sensa-tions in the body. However, it can be an unpredictable and dangerous process. Reich and his followers, many of whom were skillful practition-ers, precipitated psychiatric crises in many clients because of the profound anxiety released by too much deep, rapid breathing. For this reason I grav-itated away from Reichian-style breathing toward gentler practices that I found more effective and completely safe.

I began to find ways to apply my new knowledge to my daily life. Not long after I had discovered the power of breathing, I was roundly criticized for an administrative mistake I had made. As I drove home that day, I found myself replaying the conversation with the dean who had criticized me. Each time I replayed the conversation I would edit it slightly to include some devastating reply on my part, one that reduced him to quivering jelly. Of course, in actual fact I had stood and taken it dumbly, like a deer caught in the headlights. Suddenly I realized that my righteous anger was a way of masking the pain I felt. I took a few deep breaths into the pain. It subsided and turned into sadness. I took a few more breaths into the sadness and a question formed in my mind. Why was criticism always such a big issue for me? Why was sadness just a few breaths under the surface of it?

Then I realized that all this was really about my father. He had been ab-sent when I was growing up, and I think I keenly felt that loss, even though I never consciously acknowledged it at the time. Now, nearly thirty, I was projecting my need for my father's approval onto this little bowtied dean, who in actual fact was probably only a few years older than I was. The realization was helpful to me, but what really moved me was how quickly I got in touch with it by using my breathing as a searchlight. It was totally effortless. I just breathed a few times and wondered; the answer was right there, as if it had been waiting to be breathed on.

I also began using the searchlight of the breath in my work as a therapist. One of the great aspects of the training program at Stanford was that doctoral students were immersed in doing therapy from practically the first day. The clients paid very low fees or no fees at all. There was great freedom to experiment, because clients were told clearly that one of the missions of the counseling center was to try out innovative methods. It was here, from 1971 to 1974, that I tried out many of the techniques that would later form the heart of my system of therapy.

I would ask my clients to listen to their bodies, to notice where and what they were feeling. Then I would ask them to breathe into the place where they felt those feelings. This never failed to produce results. They would come to deeper resolutions during the sessions than I had seen before. But more important, they left the sessions with a natural tool that they could carry with them into everyday life.

I continued to have positive experiences with conscious breathing. Some of these findings seemed trivial, but they helped me learn the power of breathing in my own body. One night I went out with some friends to a Mexican restaurant. I had the deluxe combo plate and returned home later feeling stuffed and queasy. Using my new-found skills, I started to breathe into the uncomfortable feelings in my body. It became hard to do this in a chair, so I lay down on the floor and loosened my belt. For about ten minutes I simply focused on the sensations and took full, slow deep breaths down into my stomach area. Lo and behold, the sensations went away. When I got up, there was no trace of the discomfort I had felt a few minutes earlier.

Finding myself quivering with anxiety before one of my first public speaking engagements, I sat backstage and took slow, deep belly-breaths. The anxiety dissolved into energy and excitement, proving Fritz Perls's adage that fear is excitement without the breath. On the golf course I developed the habit of taking a full breath before my swing, a practice I continue into the present because of its ability to center me. I looked for any way I could find to bring the power of conscious breathing into my daily life.

In those early years I also made the discovery of Moshe Feldenkrais and his form of bodywork. His understanding of breathing and how the body functions was of great help to me. Not only did I learn from his books and presentations, but he also inspired me to watch animals and babies breathe, and to experiment with my own breathing.

Just after I moved to Colorado in 1974, one of my clients came in saying she was on the brink of an anxiety attack. She was upset about her husband seeing another woman. Her breath was laboring up in her chest, and she was showing some of the initial symptoms of hyperventilation such as tingly hands and a clammy pallor. I invited her to participate with her fear rather than trying to control it or make it go away. Her breathing escalated like a runaway train. I told her to put her hands on her belly and aim her breath down in that direction. Then I began counting her breaths with her, gradually slowing the count. Soon she was breathing at a much more relaxed rate—about eight breaths a minute—and she was feeling comfortable enough to discuss solutions to her relationship problem. This experience taught me that one should always deal with feelings and correct the breathing before attempting to solve any problem on the cognitive level. I soon had more opportunities to work with breathing (and more work than I could handle): My client, a well-connected socialite, referred a dozen of her friends to me that month, and my career as a body-centered therapist was under way.

A Bibliographical Note

THERE HAS BEEN UNTIL RECENTLY A SHORTAGE of practical, contemporary materials on breathing and the larger field of body-centered therapy. Some of the very best information on breathwork comes through oral traditions passed along by gifted teachers who are not often gifted writers. Although we are still in the early stages of the body-centered revolution, many resources are appearing or are in preparation. I will not attempt to survey the field, but rather will mention a small number of books that the serious student of breathing will probably want to read.

For an introduction to the work of Wilhelm Reich, I heartily recommend the brilliant biography by Myron Sharaf, *Fury on Earth* (New York: St. Martin's Press, 1984). It is better than any of Reich's own books at showing the evolution of his work, and it also contains a richly detailed and sympathetic look at the life and times of a true creative genius.

I cannot recommend any books by Moshe Feldenkrais, although my admiration for his work is boundless. He was, alas, not a very good writer. The tapes of his lectures and instructions are also quite uneven. He would occasionally go off on angry rants or turn peevish halfway through a lesson, marring an otherwise brilliant presentation. His students, however, have done him a great service. There are many tapes available by first- and second-generation Feldenkrais trainees. I see them advertised frequently in the pages of magazines such as *Yoga Journal*, *New Age Journal*, and *Natural Health*. I do not have a specific recommendation, but the three or four different ones I have heard are generally good. The late Thomas Hanna wrote an excellent book called *The Body of Life* (New York: Knopf, 1980), which conveys the philosophy behind Feldenkrais's work, and a workbook called *Somatics* (Reading, MA: Addison-Wesley, 1988), which gives simplified modifications of some of Feldenkrais's best exercises.

All of us in the Western body-therapy tradition walk ground first trod by the yogis of the golden age of Hindu psychology two to four thousand years ago. The ancient sages knew a great deal about breath and consciousness, some of which has survived to our time. If you would like to get to know the breadth of their knowledge, I can recommend *Light on Pranayama* (New York: Crossroad, 1985) by B.K.S. Iyengar and *The Science of Breathing* (Honesdale, PA: Himalayan Publishers, 1979) by Swami Rama and two Western colleagues, Rudolph Ballentine and Alan Hymes.

Two books from the Western medical and biofeedback traditions deserve mention. One is *The Breath Connection* (New York: Plenum Press, 1990) by Robert Fried; the other is *The Oxygen Breakthrough* (New York: William Morrow, 1990) by Sheldon Saul Hendler, M.D., Ph.D. Both of these give thorough introductions to the problems caused by faulty breathing, and both offer simple exercises that can be helpful to the beginning student.

Special mention should be made of the poetic book called *Breathing* by Michael Sky (Santa Fe, NM: Bear and Company, 1990). Sky offers an inspiring and heartful paean to the process of breathing, and his beautiful vision of the high potential of the art is an elegant and eloquent little masterpiece. If modesty will permit, I would also like to mention *At the Speed of Life* (New York: Bantam, 1993), which contains the approach to body-centered therapy that my wife, Kathlyn, and I have developed. It contains a section on integrating breathing into therapy work, along with related exercises.

APPENDIX C

Note to Professionals and Advanced Students of Conscious Breathing

BREATHWORK IS ONE OF THOSE AREAS OF INQUIRY that contains an expanding infinity of riches. After studying and practicing these techniques for years, every week brings me more insights and learning. Put simply, the more I do, the better I feel and the more I learn about breathwork's potential. The more you put these materials to work in your life—and in your practice, if you are a professional—the more miracles you will see.

We offer training programs through The Hendricks Institute on a full range of body-centered therapy skills, as well as a program on our approach to relationship therapy. The body-centered therapy program teaches you how to practice and teach the full Conscious Breathing Program, so that you can integrate it into your practice and teach workshops on it. At present we offer training in New York, California, the Pacific

Northwest, Canada, and Europe, as well as Colorado. If you would like further information, you may call us at 1-800-688-0772, or write to our director, Kathy Allen, at The Hendricks Institute, 409 East Bijou Street, Colorado Springs, CO 80903.

To supplement this book, a video version of the Conscious Breathing Program is available on VHS. Credit card orders may be placed by calling 1-800-688-0772. The cost is $25.00 plus $2.50 postage for two-week delivery. If you desire Federal Express Two-Day delivery ($10.00), please specify.

ACKNOWLEDGMENTS

I am deeply grateful to all the people who helped me discover and teach the powers of the breath. Among them:

- The late Jack Downing, M.D., who was always there for me in the early days
- Dr. Loic Jassy, valued friend, colleague, and fellow breathing-enthusiast
- The great European mind-body pioneers who influenced Reich and Feldenkrais, particularly George Groddeck
- My children, Amanda and Chris, with whom I enjoyed many conversations as I lay on the floor doing breathing exercises
- All the graduates of our training programs around the world
- Kathy Allen, director of our institute

I am doubly blessed with a literary agent and an editor who are also valued friends. Sandy Dijkstra is the agent of my dreams, and Toni Burbank is the editor every writer dreams of. To both of them, my gratitude is absolute.

Finally, I am grateful to my wife and partner, Dr. Kathlyn Thatcher Hendricks, for inspiring me each day, giving me both room and reason to breathe.

ABOUT THE AUTHOR

Gay Hendricks, Ph.D., is the author and co-author of over twenty books in psychology and education. Among his works are *The Centering Book*, *Learning to Love Yourself*, *At the Speed of Life*, and *Conscious Loving*. The latter two books are co-authored with his wife, Kathlyn Hendricks, with whom he has lived and worked for over fifteen years. Together and singly, they have appeared on many television shows, including *Oprah*, *Sally Jessie Raphaël*, and *48 Hours*. After receiving his doctorate in counseling psychology from Stanford in 1974, Gay moved to Colorado, where he and Kathlyn make their home. They have two children, Christian and Amanda.